BUDGE *on* TENNIS

BY

J. DONALD BUDGE

with

An Introduction by WALTER L. PATE
Captain, U.S. Davis Cup Team

and

A Biography by
ALLISON DANZIG
Tennis Editor, The New York Times

NEW YORK: 1939
PRENTICE-HALL, INC.

J. Donald Budge receives the James E. Sullivan memorial trophy as the outstanding amateur athlete of the United States in 1937.

Preface

"THERE WILL NEVER be another like him!" That is what the fans say about almost every tennis champion, or the champion in any other sport. The fact is that all tennis champions have something in common. One may be better than another or stand out as superior to all others, and every champion has his own peculiar style that is the expression of his individuality or personality, but each one has borrowed something from the champion before him. None can afford to ignore what has gone before him, for the past is a great teacher.

I have attempted to analyze and describe fully the technique of stroke production and the strategy of match play required by the beginner and the intermediate player to develop their games to the fullest potentialities. Since I am most familiar with my own methods and they have served me well, I am naturally partial to them and advocate them. At the same time, I feel that they should not be emphasized to the exclusion of those used by the great players of the United States and other nations during the past thirty years.

The winning game of tennis today is the fruition of the best theories and practices of the players who have served as trail-blazers. Each of them profited in turn from the advancements made by his predecessors, and each contributed something of his own to the evolution of tennis from an unimaginative, monotonous, and purely mechanical test of control between two players the length of the court apart into the fast, spectacular test of versatility and skill of today. Thus, in addition to pointing out the technique and policies of players active today, I have taken pains to familiarize myself with the methods and procedure of others who, to some of us, are only names in the record books, so that younger players can profit by their experiences.

I make no pretense to being an authority on the history and development of tennis, but from the time I became attached to it, everything connected with the game became my meat and drink. I had a keen desire not only to see all the good players, but to read about those before my time.

If you, after reading and applying the principles set down and explained here, find that they have helped you with your stroke production and have assisted you to gain a comprehensive picture of the strategy of the game, as well as to realize the vital importance of both the mental and physical processes for success in a truly great sport, I shall be deeply gratified.

As a last word, I should like to express my deep feeling of indebtedness to Tom Stow, Lloyd Budge, Walter Pate, Sidney Wood, and James Kinney. All of these, either by actual help on the court, or by the stimulus and inspiration of their encouragement, gave me assistance that I value highly and shall never forget.

J. DONALD BUDGE

Introduction

*I*T IS DIFFICULT to speak or write of Donald Budge without using superlatives, and the reader should not be surprised to meet at least a few in this introduction written by one of his ardent admirers and closest friends.

On July 20th, 1937, on the center court at historic Wimbledon, Donald Budge and Baron Gottfried von Cramm were nearing the climax of perhaps the greatest tennis match of all time. The players and all who follow the game knew that the fate of the Davis Cup hung on the outcome. In the final set Don had been desperately near defeat at 1-4, but recovered valiantly until, late that afternoon, the score board showed him to be leading by 6-8, 5-7, 6-4, 6-2, 7-6 and 'vantage point—the fifth in that dramatic game. As he took his position to serve, the huge crowd was breathless; there was utter silence. A tremendous service crashed into Von Cramm's court; those who saw were amazed at the marvelous return that kept the match alive. After a short exchange from the backcourt, Von Cramm hit hard and deep to the right corner and rushed to the net. Don's reply was a miracle shot made on the full run—a booming low forehand drive which paralleled the side line for nearly the entire length of the court—a clean passing ace. When the ball hit the ground, inches from the baseline and the same distance from the side line, the battle was over and the United States entered the challenge round against Great Britain. As it was evident that the winner of the interzone final would defeat Great Britain, Don's master stroke marked the supreme moment in American tennis since 1927, when the Cup was lost to France.

The outcome of that classic was additional evidence that Budge wins his big matches—the more important they are, the surer he is to triumph.

After losing the Davis Cup to France all our efforts up to 1937 to recover it had failed. Its return was an immediate stimulus to tennis in this country. When our team came home with the Cup, renewed inspiration was given to players to improve their games, and attendance at tournaments increased from coast to coast. The climax came at the national singles championship at Forest Hills, when thousands were turned away on the final day and Don Budge brought the national championship back to the United States. Nineteen hundred thirty-seven will long be remembered here as a banner year.

But the return of the Cup did much more than that. It inspired many of our younger players, on whom the future of tennis in our country depends, to play the aggressive, forcing type of game employed by Budge, without which the Cup would not have been recaptured. That, by far, is the most important reason why 1937 was a great year for lawn tennis in the United States.

Two of the more important objects of the United States Lawn Tennis Association are to develop character and sportsmanship, and through coaching and opportunity to play in competition, to assist promising youngsters to become first-class players. The efforts of the Association in these directions have never been so well rewarded as they were in the case of Donald Budge. The proof of his playing greatness is his record during the past two years (1937 and 1938). Here it is:

He is the only player ever to win the four major national singles championships in the same year—United States, Great Britain, Australia and France (1938). He is the only player ever to hold the men's singles, the men's doubles, and the mixed doubles championships of Great Britain or of the United States in the same year. He won all three titles at Wimbledon (championships won there are universally regarded as World's titles) in 1937 and again in 1938, and was also national champion in all three events in 1938 in the United States. In addition, during the past three years he won every Davis Cup singles match in which he engaged, and a long list of major tournaments between times. No player had ever won the "World's Title" at Wimbledon without the loss of a set in the entire tournament until Don accomplished that feat in 1938; in 1937 he lost only one set. He lost no set in winning the Australian title in 1938, only two in the 1937 United States championship, and only one in 1938. No other player ever equalled or came close to that record.

Since 1895 I have, many times, seen all the great players of the world in action and have played with and against all but a very few. In my opinion Donald Budge is the greatest player of them all and that means that I believe him to be the supreme player of all time. All the others lost important matches during their best years. Don Budge lost none. One of his outstanding traits is his ability to raise his game sufficiently to win important matches.

When the stakes are greatest, he is at his best. If there are any who disagree with me, I can only say that in nearly all branches of sport the performances of today's champions surpass those of yesterday and there appears to be no reason why tennis should provide an exception. Records continue to fall with remarkable regularity as a result of specialization and improvement in the science and technique of handling the human body, and the end is not yet. Since in all cases in which present performances can be compared with former records this steady improvement is clearly demonstrated, it seems reasonably certain that it holds true in sports in which there is no way of comparing present and past performances. For three consecutive years Don Budge has dominated tennis as few athletes have ever dominated their respective fields of sport.

Young players ambitious to improve their game should strive to learn Don Budge's tactics and stroke production. The three reels of slow motion pictures from which the illustrations in this book were taken were made under my direction. A score of "shots" were taken of all the important strokes and the best of each selected. Those that appear in the following pages are gems and illustrate exactly how the champion makes each of them. They are all orthodox and will reward careful examination and study.

Pictures of a player's various positions in making a stroke tell little, if anything, of his tactics and generalship. Perfection in stroke production alone will not make a champion. He must know how and when to employ every stroke in his repertory. Championship matches today are won only by the player who is able to "take the play away from his opponent," and this can be accomplished only by relentless controlled speed and aggressive tactics which force the player on the opposite side of the net to do most of the running and give him a minimum of time to make his returns. In the numerous important matches I have seen Don play, his opponent did most of the running and was forced, in consequence, to play defensively. The average feet-per-second speed of *all* the balls which leave his racket in an important match is, I believe, greater than that of any player who ever lived; yet his timing is so nearly perfect and his rhythm so beautiful that his movements seem effortless and he seldom appears hurried or seems to employ great physical effort in making even the fastest shot.

It was my privilege and good fortune to be intimately associated with Don Budge for four consecutive years. During that time I learned to respect and admire his character and personality as much as his tennis—modest, considerate, a perfect sportsman on and off the court, with a high sense of honor and integrity and loyalty to a rare degree.

By his prowess and outstanding sportsmanship Don Budge as an amateur rendered an invaluable service to the game. In joining the professional ranks he adds stimulus to the amateur game by leaving the field open to others. His fine influence will be felt in tennis for many years to come.

WALTER L. PATE
Captain, United States Davis Cup Team

Contents

Illustrations

The eight series of action photographs were taken from slow-motion films made for the United States Lawn Tennis Association by Harold McCracken, Courier Productions, Inc., New York, N. Y.

The Story of J. Donald Budge

By Allison Danzig

*I*N THE EVENING of November 9, 1938, telegrams were delivered to the sports editors of the New York newspapers, inviting them to send representatives to a Wall Street address, where an important announcement in connection with Donald Budge was to be made the next day. The messages bore the signature of Walter Pate.

The following noon, a score of reporters gathered in the law chambers of Mr. Pate, and the knowing smiles they exchanged in the reception hall told plainly that they were under no misapprehension regarding the nature of the information to be disclosed. Some of them, to whom the element of time was important in the transmission of front-page spot news for early afternoon editions, already had prepared their sports desks for a quick get-away by supplying them with a skeletonized story, to be confirmed by telephone and released to the presses instantly. There was not one among them who had not divined they were to be told that the world's foremost amateur tennis player was entering upon a professional career. All they wanted was the official word from his own lips, along with the terms of his contract, and any additional pertinent details.

Though the reason for their foregathering was no mystery to them, at the same time they were puzzled that they

1

had been summoned to the offices of Mr. Pate for the announcement. Devoted friend of Donald Budge though he was, still, he was the captain of the Davis Cup team and a high and influential committeeman in the United States Lawn Tennis Association. Since when, the reporters asked themselves, had the governing body of amateur tennis become the sponsor and affiliate of professional tennis? Why was amateur tennis lending the prestige of its august dignity to promote the success of an undertaking calculated to strike at its revenues and stir its resentment?

Not even the strong bond of friendship between Budge and his captain had prepared the press for any such lying down together of the lion and the lamb, but they were even more surprised when they were ushered into the room in which the stage had been set for the interview. Standing in the group behind Mr. Pate's desk was Holcombe Ward, president of the U.S.L.T.A.—a gentleman who, during the many years he has served the organization with distinction and uncompromising integrity, has come to be regarded as the particular guardian of its amateur standards.

Not only was Mr. Ward present. Along with Mr. Pate, he publicly commended the wisdom of Donald Budge's decision to close his amateur career and seek his fortune in the professional ranks, and wished him the fullest measure of success in his new role.

To appreciate the significance of the occasion, one had only to recall the attitude of cool aloofness maintained by the U.S.L.T.A. in the face of all previous withdrawals from its ranks. Further, none of them had dealt the association quite so damaging a blow as did this one.

William Tilden was in his late thirties and past his

physical peak when he forfeited his amateur status after
the close of the 1930 season. Ellsworth Vines had the
worst year of his career in 1933, prior to embracing pro-
fessionalism, though the cup might have been won back
sooner had he remained in the fold. Vincent Richards
said farewell to amateur tennis just at the time he seemed
ready to step into the shoes of Tilden, and when he might
have prevented the French from lifting the cup in 1927
had he been available. He, in addition, had not won the
championship of either the United States or Great Britain.

Budge said goodbye as the head man of all amateur
tennis, whose supremacy was as incontestable as was Tilden's in the early twenties. His loss cost the U.S.L.T.A.
its greatest box-office magnet and swung the balance of
Davis Cup power from America to Australia. If for no
other reason than that it might mean the end of the United
States' hold on the cup, which was brought back only after
ten years of perseverance, his exit from the amateur ranks
at the age of 23 was an occasion for the association to go
into mourning.

Yet, as jolting as was the blow, Donald Budge was so
highly esteemed and affectionately regarded by the executives of amateur tennis that they publicly gave their bless-
ing to his new venture even though, at the same time, they
were indirectly indorsing and giving encouragement to
professional tennis—regarded as anathema by foreign
amateur tennis associations.

It took more than Budge's restoration of American supremacy on the courts to account for the unprecedented
honor paid him on this occasion. As great a store as the
U.S.L.T.A. set on the Davis Cup and as keen as was its
satisfaction in his unparalleled conquests, these factors are

not enough to explain why the association should have taken so warm and personal an interest in his departure to what might be termed a rival group.

To get the answer, it is necessary to look behind the player and the record. There we find the warm, kindly personality of a polite, level-headed youth as genuine and unspoiled by the limelight as when he dwelt among the untrodden ways, a youth with a deep-rooted sense of gratitude and loyalty to the game that opened up a new vista of life to him. In a word, character was Donald Budge's open sesame to the more tender sentiments of a conservative governing body that had commonly been pictured as a stern taskmaster cracking the whip over transgressors of the amateur code and lacking the capacity for any such display of feeling.

It calls for a lot of character to turn one's back upon $50,000. When Budge rejected an offer for that amount as compensation for affixing his signature to a professional contract late in 1937, any number of people were of the opinion that the young man was badly in need of a business adviser with hard, practical sense. He had brought home the Davis Cup and the Wimbledon championship and won the American crown, and such was his renown that his name was worth a fortune on tour.

It was pointed out that he might never have such a big year again, that a rival might arise to challenge his pre-eminence, or that he might suffer an injury or a loss of confidence that would adversely affect his game. It was foolhardy, he was told, to pass up the chance to gain financial security for life with the stroke of a pen when it might prove to be his last opportunity to capitalize his fame and skill.

Budge was struck with the cogency of these arguments. He appreciated the risk he was taking, and the desire to contribute to the security of his family and to give his father and mother a few extra comforts in their declining years added to the difficulty he must have experienced in arriving at and standing by his decision. But, as tempting as was the offer, and as persuasive as were the reasons for his accepting it, he did not take the fifty thousand dollars. More compelling in his mind was his obligation to amateur tennis, and in the end his loyalty to the game that had done so much for him guided him to his decision.

The U.S.L.T.A. had the privilege of staging the Davis Cup challenge round in 1938 for the first time since 1927. It needed him to assist in the defense of the cup against the dangerous challenge of Australia. It was his duty to stand by, and he felt he could not do otherwise, much as he would have liked the money.

Though it smacks of heroics, Budge did not think he was a hero or a martyr. He gave no public explanation for his decision at the time. He simply made it and kept it, ignoring the caustic comment of those who, in their superior wisdom, were quite sure that he needed a nurse or a keeper. So it should not be so difficult to understand why the U.S.L.T.A. thought Donald Budge was the salt of the earth and that as a professional, no less than as an amateur, he would be a credit to the game, continuing to win converts to tennis wherever he might play through his exemplary bearing and sportsmanship as well as with the might of his racquet.

The climb of Donald Budge from small-town obscurity to world fame and to more wealth in a few months of professional touring than most mortals amass in a lifetime offers the characteristic American success story. To this self-reliant, pleasant-dispositioned young giant from a Scotch-Irish family of modest circumstances, whose father played on the famous Glasgow Rangers soccer team in his native Scotland, have befallen greater honors and the prospect of greater riches than have been the lot of any other tennis player in history, with the possible exception of Tilden. Solely through his own efforts and the sovereignty of his character, Budge has made of a tennis racquet an Aladdin's lamp that has won him world-wide renown, financial security, and titles that no other has been able to affix to his name in any one year on record.

To this young man, in his twenty-second year, came the honor of bringing back the Davis Cup after nine years of fruitless quest by the best players America could muster. Along with it, he won for himself the championship of Great Britain at Wimbledon, and of the United States at Forest Hills. To him, a twelve-month later, went the distinction of being the first player ever to capture all four of the world's major tennis crowns (the British, American, French and Australian) in one and the same year—a feat that placed him among the Olympians of sport alongside of Bobby Jones, the artisan of the grand slam in golf.

In recognition of his signal achievements, Donald Budge, furthermore, was voted the Sullivan trophy as the outstanding amateur athlete in 1937 by a tribunal of six hundred sports leaders throughout the country, the award being made on the basis not only of competitive sports performance, but also of the example and influence of the athlete in advancing the cause of amateur sportsmanship. He was the first tennis player to be singled out for this honor. The same year he was chosen in a nation-wide press poll as the foremost athlete of the country, amateur or professional, and he led all others in this poll again in 1938, the first to head the list a second time.

That so much distinction should accrue to one young man is justification enough for telling his story. Even beyond that, the story of Budge's rise to dominion on the tennis courts is unique in that it mirrors his achievement of greatness in a game for which he had no predilection. The Tildens, Richards, Lacostes, and Lenglens were tennis players by inclination; they were never so happy in their formative years as when they could get on the court.

Budge did not like tennis, to begin with, and he liked it less after his introduction to the game. It was only to please his older brother, Lloyd, that finally he grudgingly allowed himself to be led off to the courts. Baseball, football, basketball, hockey, bicycle riding, roller skating, and marbles all had far more appeal for him, and, with the aptitude of the natural athlete, he excelled in them to a degree in his neighborhood to earn a reputation among his young friends in Oakland, California. He was particularly clever in basketball, in which he was to win his letter when he went to University High, but no sport had a greater appeal for him than did football. He played football in the streets so much, joining every group of boys that came along throughout the afternoon, that his father thought he was overdoing it and at times severely took him to account. His father had suffered a bad injury playing soccer in Glasgow that nearly cost him his life and he was concerned lest his son suffer a mishap in playing when he was fatigued.

Young Donald did not devote all his play time to games.

He was handy with tools and liked to make things out of wood. As much as he enjoyed his neighborhood associations, he was not dependent upon his friends. He could be quite content playing alone and amused himself for hours with his father's tool chest, making things for himself and his sister, Jean. His days were usually well taken up and any time that he gave to tennis he begrudged.

For two years Lloyd tried in vain to win his younger brother to tennis, but the latter's interest lagged more and more, and finally he gave up the sport entirely. It was more fun to play the games he liked with boys of his own age.

For four years, from the age of eleven to fifteen, Donald did not go near the courts. Tennis was farthest from his thoughts, and his brother, madly devoted to the sport, had reconciled himself to being the sole tennis player of the family. Parenthetically, it was the irony of fate that Lloyd, the member of the Budge family who wanted, above everything else, to be a great tennis star, who gave himself wholeheartedly to improving his game, never got very far as a player, though he has had a considerable success as a coach. His younger brother, utterly indifferent to tennis until he was in his teens, was the one who was to make history. At least, Lloyd had the satisfaction of putting Donald on the track that was to carry him to Wimbledon, Forest Hills, Auteuil, and Australia.

It happened one night in June at the Budge family dinner table. The year was 1930 and Donald was nearing his fifteenth birthday. The California state boys' championship was a week away, and Lloyd, in the spirit of jest, asked his brother why he did not start playing again and beat some of the boys in the tournament.

Donald was the only one at the table who did not join in the laughter. He made no reply, but the following day he was out on the courts practicing. He was there the next day, too, and the day after, and right on through the week.

The succeeding week he was in the field that started out in the California state boys' championship, and he went straight through to the final—in corduroy pants. On the day of the final, he appeared in new white ducks, as spotless as though they had just come from the laundry which his father managed in Oakland. He played Paul Newton and defeated him by the score of 6-0, 6-4. He had won the first tournament in which he had ever competed.

The 15-year-old youngster naturally was tickled over his success, which came as a birthday present. He decided then and there that he would keep on playing tennis, and he set a higher goal for himself, something that he continued to do as he passed each successive milestone on his climb to the top. His next goal was the California state junior championship. Charles Hunt, a brother of the now more famous Joe Hunt, beat him twice in the finals, but in 1933 Budge turned the tables on him and added that title to the Pacific Coast junior crown which he had won in 1932.

The year of 1933 saw Donald step out for the first time in senior competition and he became the first player in years to win both the state junior and senior championships in the same season. Edward Chandler, a former winner of the national intercollegiate title, and Robert Riggs, destined for high honors as Budge's Davis Cup teammate five years later, were among his victims in the state championship. He also won the Del Monte, Oakland, and San Jose senior tournaments. Only once was he beaten in either division of competition, and as a reward for his striking progress, which he owed in part to the encouragement and help of his brother, Lloyd, he was sent East by the Northern California Association to play in the national junior championships at Culver, Indiana.

For the first time now they were beginning to visualize in this serious-minded, rapidly growing youngster another California Comet comparable to Maurice McLoughlin and William Johnston. The fact that he had red hair gave point to the comparison, but, unlike McLoughlin and Johnston, he was not a volleyer, nor was he an abnormally hard hitter, lacking McLoughlin's cannonball serve and Johnston's devastating drive.

Young Budge was yet a long way from being a champion. He was playing simply a steady, backcourt game, hitting everything back, and he had a dread of going to the net. Now, however, he was not playing tennis against his personal wish. Once he had decided to go in for the game seriously, he went all the way, and the strength and purpose of his character were manifest in the zeal and conscientiousness with which he devoted himself to improving his strokes. Baseball, football, basketball, hockey, and all the other games had now become "minor sports."

One interesting thing about his tennis at this early stage was the fact that he was hitting his backhand the same way he does now. His forehand was to give him no end of trouble and he changed his grip on the racquet several times before he finally worked the stroke out to his satisfaction in later years, but his backhand from the beginning to the present has always been made the same way.

He says the stroke is a natural adaptation from the left-handed swing that he used in baseball (he threw right-handed). When he first began to play tennis, he used his brother's racquets, and since they were too heavy for him, he hit with both hands on the handle, exactly as he did with the baseball bat. Even today he still supports the racquet (15 ounces!) with both hands for his backhand as he begins his backswing, but he lets go the left hand as he starts the forward movement of the racquet. The only difference between his backhand as it was in 1933 as a junior and as it is today, when it is rated the best in the world, is that originally the shot was a slice, but now he hits into the ball instead of down.

Budge's first trip eastward was a success. He won the national junior title at Culver, and the player he defeated in the final was none other than Gene Mako of Los Angeles, who was to be his Davis Cup team partner and share many notable triumphs in doubles with him, including the winning of the national and Wimbledon championships. In this match were sown the seeds of friendship between Budge and Mako, just as the strong bond between Wilmer Allison and John Van Ryn, another great doubles team, was cemented in their meeting in the final of the singles at Seabright on a blistering hot day in 1928.

Mako's affable, breezy manner and irrepressible good nature, which was likely to break out in a pun at any time in the most dignified surroundings, were to have their influence upon the rather gawky, red-haired stripling from Oakland. Budge at this time was an extremely reserved youth. Among his intimates he was entirely at ease and happy, and at University High his marks had fallen off a degree because of his love of companionship and "kidding" with the fellows, though he never got into difficulties in his classwork. But among strangers young Donald was almost painfully shy and reticent, fearful of trying to be funny lest anything he said be taken the wrong way. This was particularly true when he was in the presence of girls, and even at home he usually crossed to the other side of the street to avoid the embarrassment of meeting them.

Through his association with Mako, who never was known to be "fussed" or tongue-tied in any situation, Budge gained in poise and self-confidence, rid himself of his shyness in meeting and talking to people. By 1935 he had acquired so much self-possession that he could follow Gene's example in taking over the traps of Benny Goodman's or Tommy Dorsey's band, and Mako could call his attention, when they were playing doubles at Wimbledon, to the good-looker in Section E of the stands without Donald tripping over his feet and flubbing his next shot.

Donald did not get any farther East than Culver in 1933, but in 1934 he was judged to be ripe for the "big time" competition of the Atlantic seaboard—for the famous grass court fixtures to which every budding young player looks forward and in which he usually establishes his claim to a ranking in the country's "first ten."

Prior to setting out on his first adventure across the continent, Donald retained his California state championship, and for the first time on record he joined forces with Mako in doubles to carry off the Pacific Coast sectional championship at Santa Barbara. His trip East was broken up by a stop-over at Chicago for the national clay court championship. That the 19-year-old youngster was definitely on his way up the tennis ladder became evident when he defeated Frank Parker, then beginning to be regarded as almost invincible on clay, in the semi-finals. Bryan (Bitsy) Grant was too steady for him in the final, but he was to turn the tables on the "Mighty Atom" from Atlanta in the turf court championship at Forest Hills. Incidentally, he beat out these same two rivals when he made his debut as a Davis Cup singles player in 1935.

Budge's Eastern "unveiling" took place at the Seabright Lawn Tennis and Cricket Club in New Jersey, one of the oldest and most influential clubs in the country, whose velvet turf had been trod by every great player of the United States and most of the ablest from abroad. The best that wealth, prestige, tradition and experience could offer in the way of perfect turf and expert tournament management set the stage for the debut of the 19-year-old, red-headed youngster from the far West, as they had for numerous other hopefuls before him.

Budge's appearance created nothing like the sensation that did that of Ellsworth Vines there in 1930; but his name was becoming familiar, and those who were drawn to his court were impressed by his resemblance to Vines in his physical proportions and style of play, as well as in the poise and earnestness with which this freckled lad went about his business without asking favors of anyone. Self-reliance was written all over his thin face, and his radiant grin took in an equal amount of territory. The similarity to Vines was carried out even to the pronounced posterior waggle with which he set himself in a bent-over position to receive service. There was one point of radical difference, however; whereas Vines had shown the flat "Eastern" grip on his first visit to the Atlantic Coast, Budge was using the "Western."

William Johnston had possessed a great forehand of the

Western top-spin variety, but since his day no other player aside from John Doeg had been able to win the men's championship with a Western drive. So, despite the fact that Frank Shields and George Lott were winning high ranking with a Western, and Gregory Mangin and Berkeley Bell, also in the first-ten ranking, were using it, this grip had become more or less obsolete.

Advocacy of the Eastern grip by William Tilden and Vincent Richards was sufficient to establish definitely the vogue of the flat drive once Johnston and his forehand passed from the grass court scene in 1927. Thus, it was a keen disappointment to those who had looked forward to the arrival of this new young prospect, Donald Budge, to find that he was using the grip adapted to taking a high-rising ball on the hard surfaces indigenous to California.

Strangely enough, it was the influence of players from outside California that was responsible for Budge's adoption of the Western grip. His brother, Lloyd, had taught him the Eastern from the beginning, and he was doing very well with it and perfectly content. Then Lott, Bell, and Mangin came to Berkeley, California with their top-spin drives, and the force with which they banged the ball made a strong impression upon the youngster. He decided that if that was the way these ranking stars did it after playing on Eastern turf, that was the way for him. So he changed to the Western, and for four years he used nothing else, although he did not use much top-spin.

From the time he first came East, Donald realized the mistake he had made and how much better it would have been for him had he not given up the smooth, flat stroke he had started with originally. He discovered in his opening match at Seabright that the Western grip was not suited to taking a sliced, low-rising ball on grass, and the difficulty of dealing with the ball on wet turf was made clear to him later on.   He was put out in the second round at Seabright by Henry Prusoff of Seattle, Washington, who, incidentally, had a Western drive himself, terrifically powerful, though erratic.   Bell, with his deadly chop, allowed him only three games in three sets in the Longwood Bowl tournament, though an ankle injury suffered by Budge accounted in part for the rout, and Donald's only notable conquest of the season in the East was his victory over Grant in the championship at Forest Hills.

Dissatisfied with his showing and particularly with his forehand, Budge returned home.   That autumn he corresponded with Sidney Wood, Wimbledon champion in 1931, who had played a good deal of tennis in California with Lloyd and had been helpful on several occasions to the younger brother.   Wood advised him that the Eastern was the better grip for grass and recommended that, if he had the confidence he could hit with it, he should change to it.   The youngster had no sooner read the letter than he went directly to the courts and started to work.

Tom Stow, coach of the University of California tennis team and the Claremont country club, to whom Budge feels particularly indebted for an interest and valuable help in the development of his game, worked with him all that winter and had him change to a grip that was half way between the Eastern and the Continental.   But in the spring of 1935, while he was with the Davis Cup team in Mexico, Walter Pate, captain of the team, advised Budge to use the flat Eastern.   He tried it.   It worked beautifully, and from that time on he has used this grip, though he found it necessary to work on it each succeeding winter with the help of Wood, Stow and his brother, Lloyd. Not until 1937 did he hit his forehand with the complete confidence he had in his backhand.

The difficulty he had in mastering the forehand was one of the sorest trials of Budge's career. There were times when he was so discouraged that he asked himself whether it was worth all the worry and effort. Each time he decided that it was, and stayed in the fight.

It was in 1935, or only a year after he had played on Eastern turf for the first time, that Budge gained the stature of an international player. Vines was in the professional ranks, as also were Lester Stoefen and George Lott. Wood and Shields, though they ranked second and third, respectively, after Wilmer Allison, were passed by (at their request) in the deliberations of the committee that selected the Davis Cup team. It was decided to use new blood in the effort to regain the long-absent trophy, particularly in view of the fact that all four singles matches had been lost to Great Britain in the 1934 challenge round. Budge, although he ranked ninth, was chosen with Allison, our Number 1 player, for the singles, getting the call over Parker and Grant.

So Donald went to Wimbledon. The lad who did not want to play tennis, who refused to touch a racquet for four years and did not compete in his first senior tournament until he was eighteen, now, just barely twenty, was going to play before the Queen of England and the most critical, tennis-wise gallery on the most famous stretch of tennis turf in the world. Two years before, his name had hardly been heard of in the East, and here he was sailing for Europe as the representative of Uncle Sam in the biggest of all championships.

Was he overwhelmed with the august importance of his mission? It would have been excusable if he had been, but those who saw the team off at the pier did not gain that impression when they glimpsed the tall, red-headed youngster and his equally towering doubles partner, Gene Mako, stroll casually up the gangplank, bare-headed and in their shirt sleeves, a few minutes before sailing time. Their overseas captain, Joseph W. Wear, had just about given up hope of having them with him for the trip. They had been doing some last-minute shopping for phonographs and the latest swing music records.

Several interesting stories about the newest California tennis sensation came out of that trip. When his ship reached the other side, so one of the yarns ran, a government official knocked at his cabin. A sleepy-eyed youth with tousled red hair opened the door in his pyjamas and asked what was wanted.

"Let me see your visa," he was requested.

A look of perplexity crossed the face of the irritated young man, who did not like being disturbed from his sleep. Then a light dawned on him and his annoyance was all the greater.

"Oh, you mean my vizor," he said sharply, indignant that anyone should wake him up to make any such ridiculous request. The official was even more incensed.

"Listen, young man," he snapped, "I've been in this business for twenty years and it's visa."

The red-headed youth came right back:

"I don't care how long you've been in the business,

mister.   Out in California everybody wears eyeshades, and we call 'em vizors."

There was the story about the time he was playing Bunny Austin on the center court at Wimbledon in the British championship and the Queen entered the royal box.   The red-headed American boy, so the cabled reports related, waved his racquet to Her Majesty and received a kindly wave of the hand in return, to the vast amusement of the gallery, which took it as a typical American gesture on the part of a green, friendly youth and liked him all the more for it.   Some of the accounts went so far as to contrast the crowd's good-natured reaction with the angry resentment provoked by John Hennessey's appearance in striped flannels in 1928 at Wimbledon, where plain white is *de rigueur*.   Mr. Hennessey, who played tennis, as he did all other things, with his tongue in his cheek, forgave himself cheerfully.

Budge scoffed at the story of his informal exchange of greetings with the Queen when he got back home.

"I may have been green," he said, "but not that green. There was no racquet waving.   I did what Austin did. We both stood by the net, faced towards the royal box and bowed to the Queen.   The boys who wrote that stuff were just having some fun."

In spite of his denial, the story caught on and refused to die.   Whether Budge waved his racquet or did the correct thing, the fact is that the young man was not overawed by the occasion and he was not nervous.   By contrast with Vines, who suffers from nervous indigestion, he is an iceberg when he steps on the tennis court.   He never lets anything worry him, even if he is playing under strange conditions, as he was at Madison Square Garden in New

York in his professional debut against Vines, and he never concerned himself with looking at the draw to see whom he had to meet in the successive rounds as an amateur.

The night before his first big Davis Cup match in 1935 —against Henner Henkel of Germany—Budge went to bed at ten o'clock and fell into a sound sleep. At two A.M. he awakened and walked down the hall. As he passed Wilmer Allison's room he saw the light was on. He pushed open the door and walked in.

"What are you doing up at this hour?" asked Donald.

"What are you doing up?" was Wilmer's rejoinder.

"I'm just going down to the bathroom to get a drink," he said, yawning sleepily. "Don't know what woke me up. I was sure sleeping beautifully." The Texas veteran, to whom these Davis Cup expeditions were an old story, looked at his visitor enviously and shook his head.

"You haven't got any nerves at all," he complained. "I wish to heaven I could go to sleep before a match. It's still the same after all these years."

———◦—◦———

Young Budge gave an excellent account of himself on his first trip overseas, although he lost both of his matches in the Davis Cup challenge round with Great Britain. He defeated Austin in the British championship at Wimbledon, where the English stylist is particularly to be feared, and in the interzone Davis Cup matches with Germany, he triumphed over Henkel and won from the great Baron Gottfried von Cramm, a notable feat even though the United States had already clinched the series before this contest went on as the concluding event. When the news came over the radio that Donald had beaten the player generally ranked second only to Perry among the amateurs of the world, the delighted officials of the United States Lawn Tennis Association knew that they had a champion in the making.

The enthusiasm over Budge's victory over Austin and his success against Von Cramm and Henkel in the cup matches was dampened somewhat when Austin turned the tables on the Oakland youngster in the Davis Cup challenge round and Perry also beat him. He took a set from each of them, however, and, considering the fact that Allison, then our Number 1 player and a seasoned campaigner on the foreign front, also lost both of his singles matches, the showing of the American newcomer was worthy of high praise, though Americans naturally were disappointed that another defeat, the ninth in succession, had been sustained in the Davis Cup competition, and this time by the shutout score of 5 to 0.

Budge's game gained considerable strength from his first play abroad. Aside from the confidence he acquired from matching his strokes against the world's best and beating them or giving them a close fight under strange conditions that had raised havoc with any number of Americans competing abroad for the first time, he had the opportunity to watch Perry in action and to profit therefrom.

This was not the first time he had seen the great British player, then the world's foremost amateur. Perry had been a regular visitor to California as a competitor in the Pacific Southwest and Pacific Coast championships and there the youthful Budge had admired him from the stands. The British champion had taken a friendly interest in him and had given him advice about the game from the time Donald was sixteen.

Budge had been thrilled to have the celebrated British champion talk to him, just as he had been in the case of Ellsworth Vines. Now, in 1935, as an internationalist representing the United States, he did not stand in such awe of Perry, though he recognized him as his superior on the courts. He could watch Perry and concentrate on what he was doing instead of losing himself in star-gazing admiration.

From his close-up inspection of the great champion's play on this trip, Budge came to a realization that started him on the way to remedying the one big deficiency in his game. His ground strokes were coming along nicely, even though he was not entirely confident with his forehand, particularly in taking a low ball. He was forcing more and putting on extra pressure, rather than merely returning the ball carefully and seeking to outsteady his opponent. He had a strong American twist service and he was adding to his knowledge of tactics, but he was not making any progress as a volleyer. He was still making his stand almost entirely at his baseline and was passing up opportunities to close in for the finishing thrust that the pace and length of his ground strokes fairly begged for.

Watching Perry, Budge began to see clearly how important it is to get to the net. Perry's quickness in moving in with his stroke, instead of making his drive and then going in, enables him to get into position for his volleys where others would be a shade too late. It requires perfect, split-second timing, faultless balance, and coördination to make the approach shot the way he does.

He takes the ball on the rise and his rear foot is crossing the front one as the racquet makes contact with the ball, so that he is on his way up with his stroke. Vines, on the other hand, makes his drive with the rear foot on the ground, and it is not until the instant the ball flies from the racquet that he starts forward.

Perry showed Budge how to make the running drive to get to the net quickly and helped him on other occasions in the United States the following year. Perry's forehand is his approach shot, and Budge followed his precepts on the backhand, which is his strong side. Gene Mako also aided him after their doubles partnership had been cemented and taught Donald how to make the high drive-volley on the forehand, which is Mako's forte.

Another factor in the development of his short-court game was his defeat upon his return from Europe by Bryan Grant in the national championship. Although the match was hardly a true test, inasmuch as the conditions were marred by a heavy downpour of rain, which made it necessary to interrupt the play, Budge took the defeat keenly to heart after doing so well abroad. It was brought home forcibly to him how vitally essential it was that he equip himself with a strong volleying attack if he was to deal successfully with so indefatigable a retriever as Grant. He resolved to give himself intensively to overcoming this weakness in his game.

A second defeat by Grant at White Sulphur Springs in the spring of 1936 impressed upon him more forcefully than ever how decisive a factor the volley is in overcoming the resistance of a resolute baseliner who gets the ball back with a prudent margin of safety. For two sets Donald attacked mercilessly and had the situation so completely in hand that the gallery could not help feeling sorry for his tiny opponent. Then, with victory apparently near at hand, Budge let up as the shrewd little fellow across the net softened his strokes to slow down the pace of the match.

Instead of hitting and going to the net, as he had been doing, Budge played Grant at his own game from the back of the court. The rallies were so long and he used up so much energy trying to drive through Grant's stonewall defense that, by the time he realized his mistake, he was too arm and leg weary to carry the attack to the net. Grant took three sets in succession and won the match.

A bit of side-play that developed in this contest illustrates the poise and self-possession that Budge brings to the court and the unfailing good nature that has made him so cordially liked by his fellow players. The large crowd that surrounded the court cheered uproariously for Grant as the little "giant-killer," after being run off his feet for two sets, got into the fight with his change of pace and spin. The noisy and rabid partisanship was enough alone to have upset most players, and, with his ground strokes faltering badly against the Atlantan's slow shots, Budge was not in a particularly happy spot. The tension increased with each game as Grant drew nearer and nearer to closing the gap between them. It was obvious that the big Californian was laboring under a great strain as he endeavored to escape from the web which Grant's spinning shots were weaving about him. Sensing that he was playing into his opponent's hands, Budge hit a hard backhand drive and went to the net.

A beautiful lob came arching from Grant's racquet. It was of just the right height and depth, and it should have been a winner. But Budge, going back fast, got under the ball and smote it down with a tremendous overhead smash angled to the side line. It was a magnificent shot and Grant stared unbelievingly at the ball, as he had stared at a dozen similar smashes by the Californian in the first two sets. It was too much for the little fellow in his wrought-up state.

"You redhead!" he exploded furiously, beside himself with disappointment and despair over Budge's stunning rejoinders to what should have been winning shots.

A roar of laughter went up from the thousands standing ten-deep about the court. Budge, toeing the line to serve, dropped his hands to his hips and stared quizzically at his opponent. For a moment, as he surveyed the tiny Grant, it seemed that he was about to forget the amenities and remonstrate, and the crowd could sense his resentment. Then a big grin spread over the giant Californian's freckled features.

"I'll see you outside after the match, Bits," he called across the net, and a big chuckle rippled and gathered volume down the side lines. After that, even the loyal sons of Dixie in the gallery found it difficult to take sides against the "Yankee" from California.

By the summer of 1936, Budge was making real progress with his short-court attack, as evidenced in his victories over Jack Crawford and Adrian Quist of Australia in the Davis Cup matches at Germantown. In his meeting with Perry in the final of the national championship at Forest Hills, he was going to the net at every opportunity. So much more aggressive was his tennis with the development of his volley that Perry was the only player to defeat him on turf all season. They met twice on grass in

championship play, and Perry was the winner both times
—first in the semi-finals at Wimbledon, which went to
four sets, and again at Forest Hills.

The latter match went to five sets and Budge led at
5-3 in the fifth, with only two points standing between
him and victory on two occasions. Fatigue was the undoing of Donald. He lacked the necessary strength to
sustain his attack after establishing his advantage. His
exertions in going to the net naturally took something
out of him and, of course, the pressure of Perry's resistance had its bearing on his slump. The wonderfully
trained British champion accepted the defensive more
than is his wont and committed himself to a policy of letting his opponent's fiery attack spend its force, at which
point he became the aggressor.

The real story behind Budge's sharp and sudden physical decline, which left his admirers disappointed and puzzled that a 21-year-old athlete who lived so carefully
should give such signs of distress, did not come out.
Budge refrained from making any explanation, for the
reason that he did not want to be put in the position of
offering an alibi and withholding any credit from Perry.
He was guided by the same true sporting instinct that
Perry had shown the year before, when the British champion refrained from revealing to the press how badly he
had bruised himself when he fell heavily in his semi-
final match with Wilmer Allison at Forest Hills and was
beaten.

Back of Budge's physical letdown was the story of an
inexperienced youth's mistake in yielding to his fondness
for malted milks. During the time of the national championship Budge was staying with Mako at the Long

Island home of Walter Pate, captain of the Davis Cup team. Each night they would play cards, and then the two youths would go out and have a few malted milks. Two days before the final, Budge's stomach turned sour while he was in the midst of a practice match with Ellsworth Vines, and he attributes that and his weakening in the final to too many malted milks. He is still fond of them, and recommends them without reservation, but he doesn't overindulge before a big match.

A few weeks later, Budge and Perry met again in the final of the Pacific Southwest championship at Los Angeles, and this time the verdict was reached in the American's favor in four sets. Budge's list of conquests for the season of 1936 included his victories over Quist and Crawford of Australia, both of whom he defeated in the American zone Davis Cup final, although the United States lost the series by 3 matches to 2, Bunny Austin, Robert Riggs, and Frank Parker. He had definitely established himself as America's foremost player, and some ranked him ahead of Baron Gottfried von Cramm as the best amateur in the world after Perry.

His forehand was still not entirely satisfactory, and after the Pacific Southwest final he went to Perry and asked him to help him with it. Truly willing to help, Perry pointed out that his biggest fault was his backswing and recommended that he shorten it. Donald worked conscientiously on his drive all that winter and applied himself to improving his net attack, going in on a backhand shot the way that Perry did on his forehand.

By the time spring, 1937, rolled around, Donald Budge was ready to make his bid for world supremacy. Perry had left the amateur ranks for a professional career and so there could be no further meetings between them until Budge followed his example, but Baron Von Cramm was still in the picture to challenge the California youth for Perry's mantle, in addition to Bunny Austin of England; Adrian Quist, Jack Crawford, John Bromwich and Vivian McGrath of Australia; Jiro Yamagishi of Japan; Roderich Menzel of Czechoslovakia (now of Sudeten Germany); Henkel of Germany; and Sidney Wood, Grant, Parker, and the rapidly oncoming Riggs of the United States.

This was not a particularly great field. It did not stand comparison with the giants of the middle twenties who challenged the supremacy of William Tilden: Johnston and Richards of the United States; Lacoste, Cochet and Borotra of France; Norton of South Africa; Alonso of Spain; Anderson and Patterson of Australia; and Shimizu and Harada of Japan. Still, among this 1937 group there were three or four of the most gifted players that ever laid hand to a racquet.

Von Cramm was definitely first class; so was Austin on given days at Wimbledon. Wood in winning the championship at Wimbledon in 1931 and with his great victory over Vines at Seabright in 1930, as well as his conquests of Lott, Shields and Allison on successive days at Southampton a week later, had established himself as a master virtuoso of the racquet, and he had played a number of brilliant matches for the Davis Cup in the years following, although 1937 was to find him handicapped by illness. Crawford in 1933 had come within a set of being the first player in history to score a grand slam.

Yamagishi, this year of 1937, was to hold galleries spellbound with his sudden-death finishing shots as he sprayed the chalk marks with a touch and rhythm comparable to Cochet's. Here was one of the greatest executioners ever to strip a tennis defense naked and make the kill with record dispatch, even though his record is fairly barren of great victories. Bromwich and Riggs today stand as the two leading rivals for world honors among the amateurs, and the strength of their play in 1937 was already commanding a healthy respect.

In competition with these and numerous others of lesser ability, Budge went through 1937 without losing a Davis Cup match or any other on turf on either side of the Atlantic. Yamagishi fell before him, 6-2, 6-2, 6-4, in the cup matches at San Francisco. Crawford and Bromwich, substituting for the ailing Quist and McGrath, lost to him in the American zone finals at Forest Hills. He beat Von Cramm in the final at Wimbledon, after eliminating Parker in the semi-finals, to win the British championship. Then came the greatest match of tennis to which Donald Budge has been a party—his meeting with Von Cramm in the fifth and deciding and critically important contest of the Davis Cup interzone round with Germany at Wimbledon.

Old timers who have watched the tennis parade since the start of the century acclaimed this as the greatest Davis Cup match ever played, and Tilden, an eyewitness, agreed with them. The percentage of earned points in this contest has probably never been equalled in cup competition, and it remained for the fifth and final set to bring forth the supreme efforts of the two magnificent antagonists, with the fate of the Davis Cup hanging upon that one last chapter.

Von Cramm, who had won the first two sets, only to yield the next two, went ahead at 4 games to 1 in the fifth. He was playing the.tennis of his life and it seemed that no player that ever lived could have stood up to him.

The gallery's delight knew no bounds, for it was unmistakably devoted to Von Cramm's cause. It was not that the blond, handsome Baron was better liked or a more genuine sportsman than the American. Both of them were extremely popular and held in high esteem for their personal qualities. It was simply owing to the fact that the British, who constituted the large majority of the spectators, felt that their team, the holder of the cup, would have a better chance of defeating Germany in the challenge round the following week than it would have of turning back the United States.

With the score at 1-4, the handful of Americans present were ready to admit defeat, and the captain of their team, Walter Pate, of New York, was experiencing some of the most agonizing moments he has ever known. But, as the players changed courts at the end of the fifth game, Budge, pausing at the umpire's chair, reassured his leader. He said:

"Don't worry, Cap. I won't let you down. I'll win this one if it kills me."

Taking his place on the court, Budge launched a rally that still makes his captain choke up with excitement when he re-tells every stroke of it. Against a Von Cramm who never for a moment let down an iota in the superlative quality of his play, who, if anything, lifted his game to even greater heights in the concluding stages as the gallery gave him its encouragement, the red-haired six-footer from Oakland played like a superman, adding force to his strokes and coming in to the net more often on his first return.

The brilliance of the tennis was almost unbelievable, with the big preponderance of the points being earned rather than won on errors. The gallery, enraptured by the scintillating display to a degree that it forgot its allegiance to the Baron, looked on spellbound as two great players, taking their inspiration from each other, worked miracles of redemption and riposte in rallies of breakneck pace that ranged all over the court. Shots that would have stood out vividly in the average match were commonplace in the cascade of electrifying strokes that stemmed from the racquets of two superb fighters until the onlookers were fairly surfeited with brilliance. In game after game they sustained their amazing virtuosity without the slightest deviation or faltering on either side.

Gradually, inch by inch, Budge picked up, and the suspense was almost unbearable. Once, only a stroke stood between him and defeat. Captain Pate does not know how he lived through that moment. At last, it was over and Von Cramm, with the fine sportsmanship which won his every rival to him, came forward with a sunny smile to shake the hand of his opponent. He had lost the most important match of his life—a match that would have put his country in the position to win the Davis Cup for the first time in the 37 years of its history—and he took his defeat as nobly as he had played.

As Budge ran forward to the net and saw that smile, which hid a disappointment that must have been cruel, he thought, as he confided afterwards to Captain Pate,

"Gottfried, you certainly have got more out of the game than any player who has won everything."

The outcome of that match—and Von Cramm must have had an inkling of it at the time—in all probability was a contributing factor in the misfortune that later overtook the Baron. There is no way of proving it, but had he won that one vital point that stood between him and victory at one stage in the fifth set, the Nazi government hardly would have turned against him as it did in the spring of 1938. He would have been needed too much for the successful staging of the first Davis Cup challenge round it would have been Germany's privilege to hold on her soil. He did not get that point, and so, instead of leading the Reich's defense of the cup of 1938, he went to prison, and the Davis Cup career of one of the finest sports' ambassadors any country ever had is presumably ended, though Von Cramm is playing again, "unattached."

Whether or not he was guilty of the charge on which he was convicted and sentenced, the American tennis public will remember Von Cramm as a thoroughbred whose quiet, reserved bearing and courteous manner to all who engaged him in match play or conversation were the antithesis of the qualities fostered and exemplified by his jailors. Such was the appeal of his chivalrous deportment and that radiantly friendly smile that kindled his fine, sensitive features that more than one tennis follower devoted to the success of Budge and the United States wishes now, in view of the fate of Von Cramm, that that vital fifth-set point had gone the other way.

The fate of Von Cramm and the banishment of Daniel Prenn, his predecessor as Germany's ranking tennis player, serve to emphasize why athletics flourish so much more in the democracies than they do elsewhere. Today, in a world nervously on edge over the conflict of ideologies and undeclared strife, it is in those comparatively happy lands where republican government guards against encroachment upon civil rights in the healthy give-and-take of right and left that is found the fullest outlet of the individual urge for physical recreation. Freedom of expression translates itself not only in speech but also in action upon the field of play.

Where there is no free speech or free press, there the inclination for the lighter diversions languishes until the cry of "kill the umpire" is no longer heard in the land and the mortality of grandmothers takes a big drop. Man comes to think of his body only as a means to the ends of the state. And so, no Mercuries arise with winged heels when the spirit is in fetters, and target practice is conducted on those who rebel against the mould into which all thought must jell.

One never hears any more of Russia as a participant in international sports competition. The Rome-Berlin-Tokyo axis values athletics only so far as they contribute towards inculcating strong nationalistic feeling and developing manpower to carry guns, and to the dissemination of propaganda.

Germany, which exploited the Olympic Games in 1936 to sell Nazism to the world, crippled her Davis Cup team last year by imprisoning her leading player, who had not been an enthusiastic salesman for Hitler in his travels, and refused permission to the members of the team to participate in the American championships after they had been badly beaten at Boston by Australia in the cup matches. The world remembers, too, the curtain of silence that fell upon Max Schmeling and the suddenness with which government officials froze up on him in Berlin after his knockout by Joe Louis in the first round.

Japan, whose athletes had made remarkable strides and distinguished themselves in the 1932 Olympics at Los Angeles, turned her thoughts away from sports when the army gained the controlling hand in the government and followed up the conquest of Manchuria with the big gamble in China proper. The result was that Nippon gave up the Olympic Games awarded to Tokyo for 1940.

The decree of the Italian Lawn Tennis Federation in 1939 requiring members of her international teams to wear national uniforms, limiting umpires to members of the Fascist party, and forbidding handshaking between opponents "to avoid the weed of intimacy" is typical of the attitude of totalitarian governments towards sport.

In Great Britain, France, and the United States, athletic games continue to be played for the game's sake regardless of the sick feeling with which the world gets up each morning. Neither the specter of war nor the internal ills of economic dislocation and political upheaval have served to dull the public appetite for contests of physical prowess. On the contrary, in these games democracy finds escape from the anxieties and problems of the front page, created in large part by the powers to whom sport for sport's sake is extravagant nonsense, and child's play is squads right and present arms.

And so Budge, to whom tennis was a game to be played for the game's sake, and to be dropped when there wasn't any fun in it, refused to go to Germany in 1938—in protest against the imprisonment of his friend. He had promised to compete there, in return for Von Cramm's visit to California in 1937, but when he found that he could not play against Gottfried, he had no heart for the trip and called it off, though he went to France, England and Yugoslavia.

It was a revealing decision. It showed that this 22-year-old youth, who was known to the public only as a tennis player and an addict to swing music, did not confine his thoughts to these two interests, but concerned himself with more serious things going on in the world and made decisions for himself. That he should have taken such a stand was in keeping with the character he exhibited on the playing court, where his scrupulous fairness and courtesy to his opponents made for the best of good feeling even though he did not make the practice of "carrying" them but applied himself seriously to the task at hand without any play to the grandstand.

Another player, tempted by the honors and round of parties awaiting his visit, might have thrown his principles overboard and acted differently. Budge, full of rhythm both on and off the court, enjoys a good time as well as the next man. His white tie and tails get a frequent airing, and dancing and music are his chief diversions. But he did not go to Berlin. He came home and played his phonograph.

To pick up the thread of our story, after that thrilling and almost miraculous victory against Germany in the interzone round in 1937, winning the Davis Cup in the challenge round was comparatively a tame and colorless formality for Donald Budge and his associates. England, deprived of the services of its mainstay, Fred Perry, was conceded to have only the remotest chance of resisting the authority of Budge's racquet, and, as it turned out, was beaten by 4 matches to 1. The United States had a scare on the opening day when Parker was beaten summarily by Austin, and Charles Hare, a stalwart left-handed youth with a blindingly fast service, held Budge on even terms to 13-all in the first set, but after that the British defense collapsed.

For the first time since 1926, the United States had won the Davis Cup, and Donald Budge returned home a conquering hero. Retriever of the world's team trophy and champion of Wimbledon, it now remained for him to win the championship of his own country for the first time to fill his cup to overflowing. That he proceeded to do by going through to the final at Forest Hills without the loss of a set and then, confronted again by Von Cramm, defeating the Baron for the third successive time. Once more they met in the final of the Pacific Southwest championship at Los Angeles, and there, too, Budge was returned the winner. In his finale for the season, Donald defeated Robert Riggs in the Pacific Coast tournament after the latter had eliminated Von Cramm.

Champion of all the realm of amateur tennis, Budge was now expected to take the step that Perry had taken the year before. The world was at his feet and he could practically dictate his own terms to the professional promoters who wooed him with lucrative contracts, but he fooled everyone except the few who were in his confidence. His friends knew how deeply indebted he felt towards the game that had given him the chance to make something of himself. He hadn't let his captain down in that fateful fifth set against Von Cramm, and, having brought the cup back, he was going to have a hand in its defense in the first challenge round to be staged in this country since 1927. So, instead of signing on the dotted line, he sailed for Australia and new worlds to conquer.

Nearly everyone thought he used poor judgment in passing up the opportunity to make a fortune. Almost as many thought he was wrong to go on so long a trip instead of resting from his months of continuous competition.

They recalled the undoing of Vines. He, too, had won the British and American championships in 1932 and then taken boat for the Antipodes. The next year, his last as an amateur, he was shorn of all his titles, and his disappointing record was attributed to too much tennis. Budge, so it was predicted, would pay the same penalty for not putting his racquets in storage for a spell, he was ill-advised to go to Australia, and the United States Lawn Tennis Association could kiss the Davis Cup goodbye in 1938.

What happened in 1938 is history and made history. Donald Budge began the year by winning the championship of Australia. He won the championship of France. He retained his title at Wimbledon, going through the tournament without the loss of a set; and after he had led the United States in the successful defense of the Davis Cup against Australia at the Germantown Cricket Club, Philadelphia, he went through the American championship with the loss of only one set, to become the first player on record to win all four of the world's major tennis crowns in the space of one calendar year.

With a heart full of good will for everyone connected with it, Donald Budge said farewell to amateur tennis in the fall of 1938. Amateur officialdom showed how it felt towards him in turning out en masse, along with some 16,000 others, for his professional debut against Ellsworth Vines at Madison Square Garden the night of January 3, 1939. Contrary to some predictions, he readily adapted his game to the strange conditions of indoor play and won handsomely, as he did also against Perry in March.

Walter Pate ranks Budge as the greatest tennis player of all time, and he is confident that the world will come around to his point of view. A goodly number of people who remember William Tilden in his prime may not agree with Captain Pate, but there is no dissenting opinion about where Budge ranks as the exemplar of all that a champion should be—in sport and out of sport. The world may never see his like again—freckles, red hair, long legs, homespun simplicity, great backhand, and all—and if it does, it will be lucky.

Tennis can stand many more Donald Budges. As long as his type reaches the top to represent the sport before the world, its directors need have no concern for its future. There must be something inherently fine about a game which turns out a specimen of young manhood who is not only a great champion but has all the qualities that make for first-class citizenship.

Amateur tennis has suffered a lot of abuse of recent years, and it has been charged specifically with making bums of its players. Donald Budge is its answer and vindication.

1

My Theory of Winning Tennis

IT'S SO SIMPLE—lawn tennis. You take a racquet, hit a ball over a net, and your opponent on the other side hits it back: elemental stuff. The area into which you must hit the ball measures 39 by 27 feet. No wide open spaces there; any young fellow in good physical condition and fairly fast on his feet should be able to reach any ball landing within that space. Tennis is just child's play. How could anyone with an adult mind work up interest in anything so lacking in imagination and scope? Learning the alphabet would be about as exciting and would offer just as much opportunity for originality.

These thoughts represented my personal reaction in the years when my brother, Lloyd, was trying to interest me in tennis. I wouldn't be bothered with anything so humdrum. Even marbles was a better game. Football, baseball, and basketball were my ideas of real sports.

It was a long time before Lloyd could keep me on the court enough to show me how ridiculously wrong a conception of tennis I had. Finally, my eyes were opened to the enormous possibilities of a game that had once struck me as being simple as pie and unworthy of grown-ups, and thereafter the better player I became, the greater I appreciated the high degree of skill and intelligence required to

38

master its technique and strategic principles. The truth is that tennis yields to no other game with which I am familiar in the premium it puts upon seasoned judgment, quick mental reaction, alert reflexes, and painstaking patience and perseverance in coördinating the hand and eye to take a moving ball upon the face of a racquet. Tennis demands, too, the physical attributes of speed afoot, excellent condition, and staying power.

The great beauty of tennis is the inexhaustible variety of playing methods to which one may make recourse. Despite the fact that it has been standardized for years and the fundamentals are the same as they were forty years ago, no two champions arrived at the top with the same game. Each of them had some particular virtue or strength that set him above his contemporaries even though, in some instances, weaknesses were to be found in his game that ordinarily would have proved an unpassable stumbling block.

One player wins with his attack, another with his defense, a third with his combination of the two, a fourth with his skill in analyzing his opponents' games and concocting methods to undermine their strengths. One player wins on sheer blinding speed; another on his clever command and application of the varieties of spin. Some have become champions with a single great shot; others have excelled without such a shot but with the uniform soundness of all their strokes in conjunction with exceptional physical endowments.

Helen Wills Moody hammered her rivals into submission with dreadnought forehand and backhand drives. With such armaments, strategy and finesse were superfluous to her needs.

William T. Tilden, 2nd, was the complete tennis player. He had the greatest mastery of spin of any man or woman in the history of the game. He had a cannonball service and blinding pace off the ground from both wings. He had one of the greatest pair of legs tennis has known. He had the ideal height, shoulders, grace, and litheness of movement that no other player with the exception of Fred Perry has matched, and he was always in condition. On top of all this, he could give most of his opponents cards and spades in his knowledge of the game from A to Z. He knew all the tricks, had all the devices, and had the brain to dictate when to make use of them.

Suzanne Lenglen was the Tilden of women's tennis. She knew the game like a book. She was the epitome of grace and flowing movement. She could put the ball on the proverbial dime, such was her control, and she won not by outhitting her opponents but by beating them on position play. Rene Lacoste had nothing like Tilden's variety of strokes, but he caught up with and beat the great American champion in 1927 in spite of Tilden's devices and wizardry. He did it entirely from the back of the court with his Continental drives that never missed against any kind of spin and that kept the full length of the court with almost unbelievable accuracy.

Henri Cochet was the master of the quickly taken ball, an artist with a racquet who never strained or hurried, was always on the ball with effortless ease, and attacked with equal facility from the forecourt and the baseline. Helen Jacobs never could develop a forehand drive, but she had a chop that broke up her opponent's superior drives. Also, she defended so valiantly that she defeated players with much better attacking equipment and won the championship four years in a row. John Doeg, like Miss Jacobs, never could master the drive, although he had one of the great serves of all time and he could volley; he won the championship with a chop for a forehand.

Fred Perry had one of the finest physiques any player ever brought to the game. He was like a cat on his feet. He had an eye like an eagle, and a wonderful sense of coördination and timing that enabled him to take the ball on the run. Perry hit a sound, fast ball; he had no use for the chop, slice, or drop shot. He was wonderfully fit, and could retrieve all day without ever losing balance, and he was a world's champion.

Ellsworth Vines had none of Perry's vitality and speed around the court, but he had possibly the hardest forehand of them all. He hurled thunderbolts whether he was serving, smashing, driving, or volleying, sometimes defying the gods of chance with the narrow margin of safety he permitted himself above the net and on the lines. Wilmer Allison had the heart of a lion, and volleyed like a madman. Sidney Wood was a master of tactics and a stylist to his fingertips who could enchant the gallery when he had the touch, and lose to a tyro when he did not have it.

A Champion Makes His Style

And so it goes. Each of these champions had something distinctive. Some of them had definite weaknesses. Others defied the tenets of orthodoxy. What one might do superlatively well, another might do very ordinarily. Each of them made the most of his own particular equipment. Each one's style of play was governed by his physical make-up and by the powers of coördination peculiar to the functioning of his individual muscular processes.

It should be evident, then, that it is idle to undertake to cut a pattern for tennis beginners to fit themselves to en masse, to prescribe hard and fast methods whereby they may become champions. The pattern would not fit the individual limitations, and there would be the danger of the beginner wasting time and effort at something beyond his capacity when he could be making progress in another direction. I can tell you what I think is the best thing for me to do and how I do it, and I can prescribe the approved general theory and practice of tactics and stroke production; but each player will have to be guided by his own peculiar physical adjustment as to what he should emphasize and concentrate on in building his game.

For example, I could tell you to go out and learn a forehand like the one J. Gilbert Hall hits. Hall's forehand is one of the best I have ever seen, and I know of extremely few players, no matter how high they rank, who would not be better off if they could borrow it. All of us would like to have that forehand, so sound and natural and true from any position in the court. But we could try until doomsday and we could not duplicate it exactly. It is a stroke peculiar to Hall's physical adjustment and anyone else copying it might find the stroke unnatural and strained.

So, instead of telling you to go out and hit forehands like Hall's, I advise that you watch Hall for footwork, distribution of the weight, fluency and continuity of the swing, and timing. Then try to observe the same general style in making the stroke as it comes naturally to you. The same would apply if anyone asked me to teach him my backhand, which I do not believe is a good model for the average player but which, though highly unorthodox, is natural for me. A lot of people would have given their right arm to have had John Doeg's service when he was booming them for twenty aces a match. But John never tried to make anyone believe they could serve the same way. He said laughingly one day that he didn't know himself how he did it, that he just hit and prayed. It came to him so naturally that he never had to think about it; he had to stop and figure it out to be able to tell you just how he made it.

If, up to this point, I have appeared to be sidestepping the issue and timid about committing myself, it is simply that I do not want to be dogmatic in telling you what is best for your game when I do not know in which direction its possibilities lie. Let me proceed immediately to present my theories as to what is the winning type of game. They may not fit in with your own individual needs, but they happened to work out successfully in my own case and are offered in the belief they may be of some help.

My idea of a real champion is a player who can force and hold the upper hand in a match. There are times, however, when a player, no matter how aggressive he is, will find himself on his heels and unable to dictate the pace. Such a situation is the test of the real champion, for he must be able to force in more ways than one. If he finds that his opponent is outhitting him from the back of the court, he can take the ball on the rise and come in to the net. He doesn't rely solely on his ground strokes to do the forcing. He must be ready at any time to bring his volley into play.

It requires a lot of confidence for a champion to change his game when things aren't going his way. I recall vividly my match with Baron Gottfried von Cramm in the Davis Cup interzone tie at Wimbledon in 1937. We were tied at two sets-all. In the fifth, nothing that I tried would work as I fell behind at 1-4. I was playing the same type of game I had started. I couldn't hold him off from the back of the court, and he had given me few opportunities to get to the net, so good was his length. I realized that I must get up there, even if I had to throw orthodoxy to the winds. So, thereafter, whenever he hit a deep ball that came fairly high over the net I would step in and volley it from far back. In other words, I made my own opportunity, even if I did have to forget about correct position in the court and take desperate chances. I defeated Von Cramm 6-8, 5-7, 6-4, 6-2, 8-6.

Keep Him Worried

My game is all attack. I must force and attack my opponent's weakness rather than just push the ball back and wait for him to make a bad shot. If I possibly can, I keep the pressure on with every stroke. As soon as you relax, it gives your opponent confidence; he thinks you are tiring. If you boom the ball, he gets worried and discouraged. If he doesn't get discouraged, mark him for a champion.

It is my idea that a point should not last too long. The use of chops and slices prolongs the rallies and puts off the eventual decision. I never slice and neither does Perry. I hit a few from the back of the court and then take the ball on the rise and come in. I did not always follow this procedure. When I first started out, I relied on steadiness. No beginner should try to kill every ball. He should first get his confidence and control. After that he comes to the second stage, when he starts to add severity to his strokes from the baseline. Once he has mastered the hard drive and has the necessary approach shots, he is ready for the third stage, taking the ball on the rise and coming in to volley and smash.

As a junior, I tried to pattern my game after Vines'. I liked his hard hitting, and his free, easy, rhythmic shots. I thought it wonderful to mope around the court like Ellsworth. I became obsessed with the idea that was the thing to do.

Then I saw Perry bounding around and I changed my mind. Fred is wonderfully graceful and, like Tilden, the perfect athlete. Half his game is his condition and footwork. I saw him take the ball on the rise and get in to the net whenever he pleased. After I began to play against him, I sought to combine a little of both Vines and Perry in my game: hard hitting and taking the ball on the rise. I immediately began to walk faster under the Perry influence.

Perry is an ideal player and a good model. My own game is too risky to serve as an example. Its success depends upon full command of every shot. I would recommend rather to the beginner that he learn how to hit correctly and nicely into the corners and wait for his opponent to miss. After he has acquired accuracy and control he can let out and take more chances.

To get to the top, every player should have at least one outstanding stroke—a stroke that may come naturally only to him. A powerful forehand, backhand, or serve is the main thing, or a great volley will be a lot of comfort. A good forehand or backhand is probably a bigger asset than anything else.

My backhand is most important to me. Most players naturally hit to the backhand side, and when they force me there, I like it. At first I wanted the play to go to my backhand, but later I decided that if I was ever to get a good forehand I would have to get a lot of balls there. So I lost any mental hazard about my forehand. It is well to remember that your other strokes can get rusty if you concentrate on one and that such favoritism isn't good for your game. At the same time, it is a good thing to have an ace in the hole to fall back upon, and that is what I have in my backhand. There were times when my forehand was so bad that I would have lost a lot of matches if I had not had my backhand and service to pull me through.

No matter how good your forehand or backhand is, it should be kept in mind that in the winning game of today, particularly on grass, the volley is what you are building up to as the finishing thrust of the rally. You should not, however, go up with the idea of having to make a brilliant volley. Your ground strokes should pave the way to make the volley easy, but by that I mean only comparatively easy. Nothing is easy in tennis when you face an opponent of your class.

When you are sitting up in the stands at Forest Hills and you see a player make a wonderful lifting volley with almost effortless smoothness—the kind of volley that you would regard as a miracle if it came off your racquet—don't get the idea that he is a genius, unless you define genius as the capacity for taking infinite pains. If you went up to him after the match and asked him how he did it so easily, he would probably smile and tell you about the hundreds of volleys he missed before he was rewarded for his months and months of practice. All the theory ever put between covers cannot supplant the practice which makes good tennis players.

2

Fundamentally Speaking

$\mathcal{H}$OW MANY TIMES have you read or heard that champions are born and not made?

The genius of a poet is supposed to be akin to, or a form of, insanity, and many people have the idea that the topnotcher in every field of endeavor, whether it be poetry, sports, music, chess, painting, or military science, is a little bit "touched." If in the field of sport, the champion is said to have been touched prenatally by the magic wand of some good fairy, which endowed him with physical qualities above the normal and foreordained that he should excel regardless of anything he did or did not do.

I am not enough of a student of the arts and sciences to pass judgment on how greatness in these categories is attained. Some of the poets I have dipped into speak a language that is sometimes over my six feet, one inch, and my reaction to the rhythms of Benny Goodman is a good deal more positive than it is to the symphonies of Beethoven, Brahms, Schubert, Mozart, or Haydn.

Probably it is true that these great masters and the Keats and Shelleys had to be born with the feeling to compose the scores and odes from which so many millions get pleasure; but when it comes to matters of sport, I am prepared to be more dogmatic, and so I should like to reg-

48

ister a negative vote on the opening proposition. I will concede that some athletes are born with something that the run-of-the-mill do not have. There has to be something there to build on, beginning with a sense of coördination, and the sports champion has to have a "feeling" for his metier in the same way as the artist for the pen and brush. In tennis, we say he hasn't got the feel of the ball on his racquet when his game goes sour, and I suppose there are days when the composer's notes come out sour. But to maintain that the champion comes into the world so gifted that all he has to do to claim his crown is to grow up and let nature take its course—I'm against it. It is in contradiction to my personal experience and to the history of every tennis champion's development with which I am familiar.

Tilden, in the judgment of a good many people, is the greatest tennis player the world has seen. And yet, it was not until he had reached the age of 27 that Tilden became champion. If he was born with a genius for the game, it was a long time in coming out. He played for years around his home, Germantown, Pennsylvania, before anyone took him seriously, and the only reason why he became a great champion was that he became practically a slave to his racquet and lived on the courts, practicing hours and hours, day after day, year after year. If he had any genius in those days, it was the genius for taking pains.

What Tilden did, every other player who got anywhere in tennis did, though probably none to the same extreme degree for so many years. Henri Cochet of France, who had as much in the way of natural gifts for the game as any player on record, still had to do his "scales" in tediously long sessions for years before he was able to profit by his wonderful sense of timing and rhythm and his innate feel for the ball.

Suzanne Lenglen, ranked by many above all other women players, gave a good part of her younger years to aiming her strokes at a handkerchief placed on the court by her father to acquire the amazing accuracy that was the chief strength of her game. Fred Perry was ready to give up the game, so long did it take him to master the knack of taking the ball on the rise. John Doeg never was able to hit a first-class forehand drive, even when he won the championship, nor could Helen Jacobs, though both worked long and hard at the stroke.

Before I could get a satisfactory forehand, after years of experimenting and practice, there were times when I was ready to give up in disgust. Any number of players could be named, including Miss Jacobs, Helen Wills Moody, Alice Marble, Wilmer Allison and myself, who went to coaches for help in correcting faults and weaknesses in their strokes after they had won high national rankings and even championships.

Practice Still Makes Perfect

The moral of all this is that behind the story of every champion's success is the record of sacrifice and painstaking effort over a period of years, and that if there is any secret of success in tennis or any other sport it is hard work and practice. So let me make it as emphatic as I know how that anyone who buys himself a racquet, a box of balls, and a pair of white pants and has any idea that he is going to become a first-class player without giving the same time and effort that he would give to become a first-class pianist or violinist is only fooling himself and wasting his time. People may tell him that he has all kinds of natural ability, that he is a born player and can't miss, but wait until he catches up with them a year later.

You get out of tennis only what you put into it—and that is the first fundamental to have in mind in starting out.

The second fundamental is the mastery of the bread and butter strokes of tennis, the forehand and backhand drive from the back of the court. They are to tennis what blocking and tackling are to football, what scales are to playing the piano. It makes no difference how good you are in the rest of your game: if you haven't sound ground strokes, you are at a disadvantage.

I know that there have been instances of players who have made big names for themselves even though they did not have good ground strokes, and that in a few instances they even won championships. I am aware of the fact that Maurice McLoughlin won the crown with his service and net play and that John Doeg did also. But we know that there are exceptions to every rule, and both of these two men had to be exceptionally talented in their specialty departments to get away with it.

McLoughlin was a terror in storming the net behind his service, and Doeg's left-handed service, one of the two or three best of all time, was so demoralizing that it constituted a mental hazard for his opponent. The latter was always harried with the thought that if he ever lost his own service, the set was gone, so seldom was anyone able to break through Doeg's. The story goes that in a Davis Cup test doubles match between Doeg and George Lott, and Tilden and Frank Hunter in 1928, Hunter, in the right court, never was able to return Doeg's service safely once in an entire set that went to 12-10, so cleverly did Doeg place it and so sharp a break did it take from the corner.

Many instances could be cited of players who might have gone much farther had their ground strokes been up to their strength in other departments. Frank Shields is one, Gregory Mangin is another, and Berkeley Bell is a third. Shields had a great service as did Doeg, and he was a pretty fair volleyer, but his ground strokes were not the best, though I will grant that against John Bromwich of Australia in the 1938 national championship his top-spin forehand was surprisingly good.

Mangin was one of the quickest men on his feet I ever saw and his reflex action was breath-taking. Also, he was a bulldog for hanging on and taking punishment in tearing to the net. But he couldn't hit a forehand, and that weakness stopped him from getting to the top despite his ambition and confidence. The same was true of Bell. He was a scrapper from the word go. He had a whistling service, like Mangin; he stormed the net and fought his heart out in every rally. But, though he had a vicious chop, he couldn't drive from the forehand and his backhand was only fair.

On the other hand, there was Molla Mallory who had no service and no volley to speak of, but had a savage forehand that won the championship for her seven times. Helen Wills Moody was not a particularly good volleyer and her footwork was not of the best, but so strong were her ground strokes that she is generally ranked the greatest woman player America has produced.

So the first resolution the player starting out in the game should make is that he will concentrate on developing a forehand and backhand drive, regardless of anything else. Everything else is secondary and can wait on the building of the ground strokes. The volleying attack is highly important and will be considered in later pages, but the success of any volleying attack is predicted by the efficiency of the drive in paving the way for the safe approach to the net. You can get there behind a strong service, but that is only in alternate games, and it takes so much out of you to deliver a strong service and rush in at the same time that not every player can keep it up very long.

Few players are able to achieve equal strength on both their forehand and backhand, and one of the early decisions you must make is which side you will favor. As I have recommended earlier, it is a good thing to have one particular shot that you can fall back upon as your ace in the hole in an emergency. It may be your service, your volley, or your forehand or backhand drive, but as a rule it will be either one of the latter two.

Don't Be a One-Shot Artist

In making this recommendation I wish to emphasize that you should not concentrate on any one stroke at the expense of the rest of your game. That is fatal, for you expose weaknesses that your opponent is sure to exploit if he plays with his eyes open. You must not neglect any part of your game and particularly you should not allow yourself to become one-sided in your backcourt play. While you may be able to run around your weak side and take the ball on your strong wing, it is difficult to do so against a strong opponent and few players are able to put on so much pressure with their strong shot as to compel the return to come back in the same line. But at the same time, while giving full consideration to all of your weapons, it is advisable to devote extra time and effort to one of them as your ace in the hole.

As it happens, my forte is the backhand. With Ellsworth Vines, Fred Perry, and most players, it is the forehand. The majority of players find it easier to make the forehand. You can make your own decision according to which comes more naturally to you. It is a good thing to remember that you should do everything in tennis as naturally as possible. This naturalness gives you more confidence, and involves less strain; consequently, your strokes do not take too much out of you and waste energy that you may need to pull through a tight match.

Another fundamental of a winning game is the volley. It is a little bit modern to rate the volley as one of the basic shots. Not so long ago it was regarded as an auxiliary to your ground strokes, to be used if you happened to have it in your equipment, but as not necessarily important to your game. This attitude prevailed until recent years despite the fact that the volley has been in the game almost from the start and was exploited brilliantly and liberally by many of our champions.

Expert opinion today attaches far more consequence to this weapon, considerably more than it did when Tilden was holding forth invincibly. Though Tilden was not a great volleyer, he was a lot better than he was given credit for, and his exhibition against Rene Lacoste in the final of the 1927 championship showed that he was more proficient than most of his contemporaries.

Nevertheless, Tilden was not in the same class with Vincent Richards and William Johnston, his chief American rivals, in the mastery of the volley, and Cochet and Jean Borotra of France made far more capital of it than he did. He was not an ardent advocate of the short-court attack. He was obsessed with the necessity of impressing upon the younger generation the vital importance of good ground strokes. That was certainly not bad advice, for one can hardly stress ground strokes too much, and who had better ones or offered a better illustration of the dividends they paid than did the invincible Tilden? But, according to present thought, Tilden did not go far enough; and since his opinion was holy writ as the champion of champions, the volley was not recognized as one of the fundamental shots.

Today, every outstanding player in the game is a volleyer. He may not be a great one, but he makes ample use of the shot and takes to the net at every opportunity. Vines, Perry and I among the professionals, and Gottfried von Cramm, Bobby Riggs, John Bromwich, Sidney Wood, Gene Mako, Adrian Quist, Wilmer Allison, Bryan Grant, Frank Parker, Joe Hunt, Frank Shields, Wayne Sabin, Elwood Cooke, Jiro Yamagishi, Franjo Kukuljevic and Franjo Puncec all are good volleyers and some of them are exceptionally fine.

The diminutive Grant illustrates the trend in the game. It wasn't so long ago that Bitsy was a backcourt pusher who spent his afternoons running his heart out with that wonderful defense of his. Then he decided to add more force to his ground strokes and make the other fellow do some of the running. That wasn't enough. He wasn't getting anywhere. So, lo and behold, the Atlanta Atom turned into a net player, and a good one. A lot of people got a laugh at seeing Bitsy go to the net, and they tell of the time that he rushed in to volleying position against Shields at Seabright after throwing up a deep lob, and Frank complained because he couldn't see the "little shaver" for the net and didn't know where to return the ball.

Grant became a volleyer because he had had his fill of being a retriever and running himself to exhaustion in long rallies. He decided that the points were lasting too long and that he would shorten them by going to the net, since he did not have the force to put the ball away from the back of the court. And there you have the answer to the reason why the volley has become a basic stroke.

It shortens the rallies and enables you to save energy instead of becoming arm weary in drawn-out exchanges from the baseline. Your ground strokes today are the instrument for paving the way for the volley, which has become the finishing shot. That doesn't mean that the drive is any less important or that it should be held in any less respect. On the contrary, it means the drive must be all the better. It must be strong to give you safe access to the net, and if you are going to the net more often you must make more good drives. Instead of lying back, exchanging a dozen or more ground strokes with your opponent, and waiting for him to miss or to give you a short ball that is an invitation to come to the net, you make your own opening for the volley with a few well-directed drives, take the ball on the rise, and set sail for the finishing thrust up forward.

The service naturally is one of the fundamentals of tennis. It is the starting point in each rally and it often decides who gets in the first telling blow, if it does not win the point outright. A good service puts you off on the right foot in that it reduces the potency of your opponent's return. It can restrict his target, compel him to play to your strength, give you a setup for a forcing blow, or afford you safe passage to the volleying position. A weak service, on the other hand, permits your opponent to strike the first telling blow and thereby gain the commanding position, if not win the point forthwith. The importance of the serve is so obvious that there should be no need to dwell upon it.

Poor Footwork Can Be a Stumbling Block

Footwork, timing and the matter of keeping the eye glued to the ball are other fundamentals of winning tennis.

Footwork is not so much a matter of speed as it is of facility and agility in the disposition of the feet so as to enable you to make your stroke smoothly and to get the full weight of your correctly balanced body behind it. More shots go wrong because of faulty footwork than for any other reason, though failure to keep the eye on the ball is a fairly close runner-up with beginners. It is not necessary to be a toe-dancer, but the player who is back on his heels, who is slow and awkward in setting himself properly to take the ball in the right position and carry forward his weight with the movement of his racquet is going to mess up a lot of shots that should have been winners.

As a general rule, the player faces the net as he waits to receive the ball. If he is to take the ball on his right side, he carries the right foot a step back in a quarter turn of 45 degrees so that his left foot is pointing towards the net and his right foot towards the sideline. At the same time, he swings his racquet back to be ready to take the ball, and places his weight on his right foot. As the ball approaches, his body inclines forward with the forward swing of his racquet, and his weight is transferred to his left foot as the racquet meets the ball approximately even with, or just ahead of, his left hip, which is parallel to the net. If he is to take the ball on his left or backhand side, it is the left foot that he carries back in a quarter turn. The matter of footwork will be considered in connection with the technique of stroke production in the chapters that follow.

Not every champion has perfect footwork, and while some may be able to "get away with" poor footwork because of their touch, none of them can afford to ignore the position of their feet when they are in a tight match. The resultant errors are too costly. You will usually find that when the top-notchers are in a slump and their control deserts them, the answer can be detected in a scrutiny of their footwork.

William Tilden and Fred Perry are almost matchless in their footwork. I should say that almost half of the strength of Perry's game lies in the wonderful quickness and sureness of his feet and his general physical condition. Suzanne Lenglen was a ballet dancer on the courts, and the perfection of her footwork was in no small part responsible for her almost incredible accuracy.

Timing is concerned with the contact of the ball and the racquet at precisely the exact instant to achieve the fullest effect of the stroke. If the ball is struck a fraction of a second too early or too late, the stroke is marred and may be ruined, though not necessarily so. Timing is particularly vital on a delicately turned shot such as the half volley, but it is important in the making of every stroke. It is just as important in tennis as it is in baseball. If the batter strikes too soon, he either misses entirely or hits the ball a glancing blow. If he swings too late, the ball smacks into the catcher's glove.

Timing is closely bound up with footwork, and, like good footwork, it is best when it is instinctive. It comes with experience, but no matter how long you have played you won't have good timing with poor footwork.

To keep the eye on the ball is about the first thing a tennis player is told when he starts out. To be hit, the ball must be seen, and obviously your timing is going to be thrown off if you don't glue your eye on the ball as it comes in to your racquet.

I don't think I need to waste any time on what is so self-evident and a stock dictum in all ball games. I will merely point out that it isn't as easy to do as it might seem, and that it calls for a real effort in concentration. Make it a habit to keep your eye on the ball from the very beginning and you will avoid a lot of grief.

3

Coming to Grips

PREPARATORY TO TAKING his first lesson in hitting the ball, the beginner comes face to face with the question of how to hold the racquet. To the uninitiated this might seem to be a trifling matter. He jumps to the conclusion that he simply takes hold of the handle, gets a grip on it that feels right, and his problem is solved.

There is a lot of sound common sense in this attitude. It amounts to the belief that you should grip the racquet in the way that seems natural to you—and anything that is natural is desirable. A natural grip makes for ease, smoothness, and the elimination of strain, and so it helps to give you confidence, which you need in tennis or anything else you do. But it is not quite so simple as that, even though you should never use a grip that is unnatural and causes you misgivings.

Tennis, unfortunately, is not played on a standardized surface. While the vast majority of players throughout the country have never seen anything but a dirt or clay court, there are other types to which they will have to adapt themselves if they have any serious ambitions for a career as a tournament competitor. There are the asphalt and cement surfaces that are common to California. There are the quick-drying composition courts that have become popular in all sections during the past decade, and, particularly, there is turf. It is upon grass that the most important tournaments, including the major national championships and the Davis Cup matches, are conducted.

On each of these different types of court the ball reacts differently from contact with the surface. The height of the bound, the speed with which the ball comes off the ground, the weight of the ball, and its receptivity to the various kinds of spin are all affected.

The height of the bound is of particular consequence, and players transferring from one surface to another may have no end of trouble in adapting themselves to the change, according to the type of grip that they are using. Ordinarily, a grip that is suited to taking a high-rising ball will not serve as effectively in dealing with a low one. On clay, dirt, cement, and asphalt surfaces, the ball gets lighter the longer it is used, whereas on turf it absorbs moisture and becomes heavier.

It can be appreciated, then, how important it is that the player select a grip that will enable him to play his game under any conditions. The progress of my own game was retarded considerably by my adoption of the wrong one, and I had no end of difficulty before I could straighten out my forehand drive, about which I will have more to say later.

It is not necessary that you change your grip for each type of court, nor is it advisable. The thing to do is to choose your grip and stay with it. Make your strokes standard, and once you are satisfied and confident that you are hitting the ball in the way that is best for you, keep on hitting it that way. If you have ambitions to make a name for yourself in tennis, I advise that you use the grip that is generally favored for grass and which has the merit of being serviceable for the other types of surface as well. I refer to the so-called "Eastern" grip.

The Eastern is one of three grips that are extensively used. The other two are the "Western" and the "Continental."

Experts Favor the Eastern

The Eastern, advocated by expert consensus, is familiarly known as the "shake hands" grip. For the forehand stroke, you take this hold by "shaking hands" with the handle, with the racquet head standing on edge and the face vertical to the ground (Picture 1). The palm and the face of the racquet are in the same plane. The wrist is behind the handle, which enables you to get extra power into your shot and makes for flexibility and a wider reach.

The grip for the backhand calls for a quarter turn of the racquet handle to the right (Picture 2). This brings the palm on top of the handle, instead of flat against the side, and at right angles to the face of the racquet. The ball is struck with the opposite face of the racquet from the one with which the forehand is made.

The Continental is approximately the Eastern backhand grip, the only difference being that you make slightly less than a quarter turn of the handle to the right from the Eastern forehand to arrive at it (Picture 3). The wrist, instead of being behind the handle, is above it. The Continental grip is the same for both the forehand and the backhand.

To take the Western grip, make a quarter turn of the

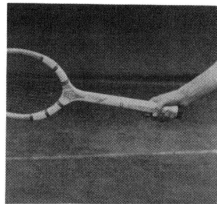

1.—Eastern forehand

2.—Eastern backhand

3.—Continental

4.—Western

THE STANDARD GRIPS

Photographs 1 and 2 by Harold McCracken
Photographs 3 and 4 by Times Wide World

Wimbledon, 1937: Kleinschroth (German captain), Pate (U.S. captain), Von Cramm, and Budge.

The U. S. team wins the Davis Cup, July 28, 1937—Budge, Frank Parker, Captain
Pate, Bryan Grant, and Gene Mako. *(Times Wide World)*

handle to the left from the Eastern forehand grip, or in the opposite direction from which you turn it for the Continental (Picture 4). That brings the wrist in line with the face of the racquet. The backhand is hit on the same face of the racquet as is the forehand, whereas the Continental backhand is hit on the opposite side from the forehand. The Western grip is also the same for both forehand and backhand.

The Western grip, adapted to taking a high-rising ball on the asphalt surfaces of the West Coast, has been losing favor of recent years. While great power can be generated with it in swooping down on the ball, and it facilitates the imparting of heavy top-spin, which helps to keep the ball in the court, at the same time it has definite drawbacks. It does not permit of the wide reach into the corners that is possible with the other two types, and the excessive over-spin that its exponents generally apply to the ball, while conducive to safety, results in a loss of speed. You can, however, hit the ball flat with the Western grip and you can slow up the speed of the shot with top-spin with the Eastern grip. But the chief objection to the Western is the fact that it handicaps the player in taking a low ball on turf; and when the grass is wet, his difficulty is aggravated.

William Johnston was the last men's champion who had a really first-class Western top-spin drive. George Lott had a good one, and John Hennessey, Frank Shields, John Doeg, Gregory Mangin, Berkeley Bell and Dr. Cranston Holman used it, but Tilden's influence turned sentiment against the Western. Despite the fact that Mrs. Helen Wills Moody hits a Western drive, this stroke has definitely lost its vogue among the men.

The players reared on the asphalt and cement courts of California, particularly from southern California, are arming themselves with the flat, Eastern drive or a modified Continental. Ellsworth Vines, Lester Stoefen, Keith Gledhill, Robert Riggs, Gene Mako, Joe Hunt, Wayne Sabin, Elwood Cooke, Jack Tidball, and Sidney Wood, a native of New York who developed his game largely in California, are examples.

I was an exception in that when I first came East I used the Western grip. However, when I started out in the game, my brother, Lloyd, taught me the Eastern. I changed to the Western, and I lived to regret it as a big mistake.

Odd as it may seem, it was watching players from the East, the Middle West and Texas that made me discard the Eastern. I was so impressed with the severity with which Gregory Mangin, George Lott and Berkeley Bell hit the ball with their Western drives when I saw them in California that I decided that was the grip for me. I used it for four years, including 1934—my first in the East—but once I had a season of grass play behind me and realized how badly equipped I was to handle a low ball on turf, particularly against a low, skidding chop, I went home and set about changing back to the Eastern. I have used it ever since.

Strong Wrist? Try the Continental

Another reason for the decline of the Western grip was the rise of the Continental. The French school of tennis became the vogue with the success of the Four Musketeers in wresting the Davis Cup from the United States in

1927. Rene Lacoste, who defeated Tilden twice in 1927 —in the cup matches and again in the final of the national championship at Forest Hills in one of the greatest matches seen in this country—and Henri Cochet became the apostles of the new style of stroke production, and "the Continental" was a great success as a grip before it became a song hit of the nation.

Karel Kozeluh, the Czechoslovakian, was being talked about, around the same time, as the greatest player in the world, although he was a professional and there was no one in his group abroad to put him to a test. He, too, used the Continental. So its vogue grew and spread, and, with the rise of Bunny Austin and Fred Perry of England, further impetus was given to its popularity.

Perry really sold it, if it needed any more selling, when he held world sway, and Mercer Beasley, who had won international fame as a coach, came to the decision that the Lacoste system of tennis was the winning game of the day and made another effort to solve the forehand difficulties of his star pupil, Frank Parker, by giving him the Continental grip. Parker did not get the results with this grip that did Perry, Lacoste, Cochet, Kozeluh and Austin, and one of the main reasons was that he did not have the great strength of wrist that it requires. Kozeluh had a wrist like a Samson, and Perry's is wonderfully strong, too.

That is one of the disadvantages of the Continental—so much effort is required of the wrist to get pace off the ground on the forehand. Another criticism to be made of it is that the tendency to hit under the ball, thus reducing the margin of safety, makes it a little bit risky. On the other side of the ledger, the player using the Continental does not have to change his grip for a ball to either side and it permits him to reach out wide for the ball on both wings. Particularly in its favor is its adaptability to taking the ball on the rise. This adaptability is valuable in the game of today, and makes for more speed, more pressure on your opponent through acceleration of your return, and quicker and safer access to the net for a volleying sortie.

Nevertheless, in spite of the adaptability of the Continental to taking a rising ball, and with all due respect to Fred Perry and the wonderful record he made as world's champion, I personally advocate the Eastern as the best of all grips for the beginner and for the finished player. I favor it particularly because it lends itself to taking both a low ball and a high ball, on turf, clay, cement, asphalt, composition or any other type of surface. I like it also because it permits of the use of tremendous power, and of hitting the ball either flat or with top-spin. I like it, too, because it is less risky than the Continental, and the flat drive with which it is synonymous picks up more pace off the ground than does the typical Western drive with its heavy load of over-spin, which gives a sharp drop to the ball.

The only disadvantage of the Eastern is the fact that you have to change the position of your hand for the forehand and backhand. But so little effort is called for to make the change that it is of negligible consideration. You do it instinctively after a while. In making the turn of the racquet for the backhand shot, I place my thumb along the back of the handle, instead of curling it under. This makes for better balance and support, and helps you to control the stroke. I recommend that the beginner try this thumb position.

Among the players in recent years who have used the Eastern grip are William Tilden, Ellsworth Vines, Vincent Richards, Sidney Wood, Wilmer Allison, Lester Stoefen, Frank Hunter, Clifford Sutter, Robert Riggs, Gene Mako, Bryan Grant, Frank Parker, Joe Hunt, John Van Ryn, Wayne Sabin, Elwood Cooke, Hal Surface, John McDiarmid, J. Gilbert Hall, Jack Tidball, Keith Gledhill, Fritz Mercur, David Jones, Donald McNeill and Junior Coen. They take in pretty nearly everyone who has ranked in the first ten during the past decade, with not more than half a dozen exceptions. That should be fairly convincing evidence of the worth of the Eastern grip.

4

The Mechanics of the Drive

$\mathcal{I}$N THE MECHANICS of stroke production, we must give first consideration to the drive. I have already stressed the vital importance of ground strokes in any winning game, and they will bear further discussion here before I go into the technical analysis of how they are made.

Tennis authorities may have conflicting opinions on various aspects of the game, including court tactics, grips, training methods, and the variation of spin; but on one point they are unanimously in accord, and that is on the primacy of the drive. This has been the case throughout the whole history of tennis and no one has arisen with new theories and principles to make them change their opinions about the drive, which has stood like Gibraltar against all innovations.

It is not difficult to understand why so much weight should be attached to the basic ground strokes. Practically three out of every four shots that you make in a match are hit after the ball has struck the ground, even if you are an accomplished volleyer. If you do not make a practice of going to the net voluntarily, the proportion will be considerably higher.

The importance of ground strokes to the nonvolleyer is obvious enough, but they are of just as much consequence to the player who carries the attack to the net. To get into volleying position, he must have the shots from the back of the court that will pave the way for his advance. They constitute the artillery that lays down the barrage before the infantry goes over the top.

Understanding, then, the value of the drive, the beginner should bend all his energies to perfecting himself in this department of the game. It should be his sole concern in the preliminary stage, and not until he has made definite progress with the drive—the foundation of his game—should he give serious consideration to anything else. I cannot stress too much the importance of laying the ground work of your game carefully; the development of your whole game may be retarded through failure to give the necessary thought and attention to the fundamentals.

Most of the champions of tennis have experienced keen anguish and discouragement with their ground strokes. With many of them, strangely, it has been the forehand. It is often true that on one side they might have clear sailing from the start and on the other they may never feel entirely satisfied. Seldom are they so fortunate as to iron out all their problems and arrive at the perfection of execution and the equality of strength on both the forehand and backhand that Tilden had.

Perry was discouraged almost to the point of giving up the game before he solved the knack of taking the ball early, but after that he went on to master it to the degree that he has one of the greatest running forehands tennis has seen. Allison was disgusted with his forehand and appeared to have gone as far as he could ever hope when Mercer Beasley helped him to straighten out the stroke.

Then he went on to win the championship. Wood, whose backhand represents the acme of style, never has been entirely pleased with his forehand and even after he had won the championship at Wimbledon he continued to experiment with it and try out something a little different each year.

In my own case, too, it was the forehand that gave me a headache. My backhand was never any worry. It came naturally from the start. But my forehand was a problem and it was not until 1937 that I really felt confident with it.

My troubles all went back to the fact that I used the wrong grip for four years. Originally I had used the Eastern, but then I changed to the Western, and when I came East for the first time in 1934 and played on grass I realized the mistake I had made. At the beginning of 1935 I went back to the Eastern, and I have used it ever since, but it required two years before I was able to get satisfactory results with my forehand.

I had a lot of anxious moments in my first season with the Eastern grip. When we were practicing for our match with Germany in the Davis Cup interzone round in 1935, I was pretty blue over the way my forehand was going. I was either underslicing the ball or I was hitting it too flat. I tried to impart a little over-spin, and in making that change I began top-spinning too much. My shots lost speed. So I attempted to flatten them out, and I began to underslice them again. I couldn't find the happy medium.

In the 1936 final of the championship at Forest Hills against Perry, my forehand was still not working any too well. It was yet only a fair shot and I didn't have confidence in it, although it was my physical condition more than any weakness of stroke that licked me. But by the next summer my forehand suddenly began to work and against Von Cramm in the final at Wimbledon and again in the Davis Cup matches that year—1937—it was functioning so satisfactorily that I enjoyed getting the ball there. Whether it came low or high made no difference to me. I had the feel, the touch, and just the right amount of over-spin to control the ball without sacrificing speed.

It was in the 1938 final at Wimbledon against Austin, however, that I definitely felt that my forehand had "arrived." It was just as good as my backhand, if not better, for it stood the brunt of Austin's attack. I was very pleasantly surprised with the way it functioned when Austin came to the net. I got off some passing shots that I didn't think I could quite make, and my average of 40 placements to 36 errors furnishes an idea of how my forehand helped me defeat Austin 6-1, 6-0, 6-3.

My backhand stroke, which is exactly the same swing I made in batting a baseball left-handed, has always been the same. When I first began to play tennis I sliced my backhand all the time, but then I learned to hit into the ball instead of down. I made the change about 1931 when I found that you could hit down with new balls but that as soon as they got lighter they would float away.

My backhand is unorthodox and peculiar to me and I don't recommend it generally as a model for beginners unless they have played a lot of baseball and hit left-handed. Yet, I never saw one that I liked any better and I have always felt that I could hit the ball the way I wanted. But no matter how satisfactory a stroke is, it can go wrong if you don't concentrate on what you are doing. I remember vividly losing confidence in my backhand on my first visit to Wimbledon.

I played Norman Farquharson of South Africa and, though I won the match, I was disgusted with myself. It wasn't good tennis. I wandered around wondering what had been wrong with my backhand. As I passed one of the outside courts, I saw two elderly women playing. Immediately I was attracted to the way one of them was hitting her backhand. She was doing it perfectly, and in a way that revealed to me what I had been doing wrong.

I had been hitting inside the ball and slicing it, instead of getting outside the ball and hitting right into it, as she was doing. I hurried to find someone to practice with. Gene Mako went out with me, and it was a wonderful feeling when I started to hit my backhand like a rifle shot.

But enough of this digression; let us study the mechanics of making the drive, and see just how the stroke is produced from beginning to end.

Before the stroke can be made, you must be in position to bring your racquet in contact with the ball. First, there is the position in which you wait for your opponent's shot. Next, there is the stance you take as you prepare to bring your racquet into play. Third, there is the position in which you actually make contact; and, fourth, there is the position at the finish of your stroke after the ball has been sent on its way.

The Forehand Drive

In waiting to receive the ball from your opponent, you stand near the baseline with your body facing the net. You should be leaning forward slightly with your weight on the balls of your feet, and with your eyes fixed on the ball (Picture 1). As the direction and length of your opponent's shot are disclosed, you move swiftly to get into position if you are required to take more than a step or two to reach it.

Personally, I like the side-skipping method, which enables me to remain facing the net and to keep my eyes on the ball. However, if I have not anticipated its direction and length quickly enough, or if I have been forced wide to one side and a burst of speed is necessary to get across the court in time to meet the ball, I turn and break into a run.

Your approach to the ball should bring you to a position about five feet in back of where you judge it will strike the ground (although this distance will vary according to the stroke), and approximately an arm's length inside the line of its flight. Your arrival at the spot should be timed ahead of the ball's contact with the ground so as to permit you to take the correct stance for making your stroke, although there will be occasions when you will be so hurried that you will have to make your swing on the dead run.

Assuming that you have skipped into position before the ball pitches from the ground, bring the right foot back in a quarter turn of the body to the right preparatory to making your forehand drive. Your right foot is now pointing towards the sideline and your left foot almost towards the net (Picture 2). It is similar to the position a baseball pitcher takes to facilitate the transfer of his weight and get the full power of his body behind his throw.

As you take this side stance, with your weight on your toes, you begin your backswing. As the racquet head goes back, the weight is shifted to the right or rear foot (Picture 3). Then the forward stroke begins. As the racquet starts to come forward, the weight of your body goes along with it and the knees are bent to permit you to get into the shot without strain or stiffness (Picture 4). At the moment of impact the weight is squarely on the left foot (Picture 5).

Correct weight-shifting makes for a rhythmical, fluent stroke and a smooth follow-through, essential for the application of top-spin, perfect control, and the maximum pace. Poor footwork, which is one of the commonest faults in tennis, and the failure to shift your weight properly can mar your timing and detract from the strength of your shot, if not ruin it entirely.

At the end of your stroke, which continues on after contact with the ball in the follow-through (Pictures 6 and 7), you come back to a position facing the net (Picture 8). Your weight should be shifting forward to your toes, so that you will be prepared to follow the shot to the net for a volley, or to move to either side quickly for your opponent's return and make your next drive.

Having discussed your position in the successive stages of making the drive, we may further analyze the stroke itself and note the position of the racquet at each stage of the swing.

There are two schools of thought as to the length of the backswing. The Continental school, of which Perry is the exemplar today, favors a short backswing. Tilden was the exponent of the long one, and so was William Johnston.

1

2

3

4

THE FOREHAND DRIVE
(Over)

Photographs by Harold McCracken

5

6

7

8

THE FOREHAND DRIVE
(Continued)

Photographs by Harold McCracken

The purpose of the backswing is to get up momentum for the forward stroke, as well as to bring the racquet head in line with the ball, and the farther the racquet travels the more momentum it should gather. But, on the other hand, something of the element of surprise is lost in using the long backswing, which fails to conceal the direction of the shot as well as does the short one; and it is not quite as desirable under pressure because of the extra time it requires. While I am partial to the long backswing (which was the one I was taught from the beginning) because of the greater security in control it seems to give, I believe that there are times for both of them according to the circumstances.

Tilden's backswing was made with a straight, sweeping backward movement. Johnston used a circular motion characteristic of those who employ the Western grip. I follow Tilden's style, except that I start the racquet back with a slight upward motion (Picture 3), instead of straight back, and straighten it out at the maximum length of the backswing.

The racquet head is brought forward in a straight line at the height at which the ball is to be taken. At all times the arm is relaxed and extended at full length (Picture 4), which is the distance at which the ball should be hit from the body to assure that the stroke will not be cramped. The wrist, slightly bent back on the backswing (Picture 4), straightens out as the racquet meets the ball at a point slightly ahead of the left hip (Picture 5).

On the flat drive, the face of the racquet is vertical to the ground at the moment of impact. If top-spin is imparted, and it is imparted to at least a small degree on almost all ground strokes that are not chopped or undersliced, there is a slight bevel or forward inclination of the upper edge of the racquet head as the ball is hit.

The racquet, moving in a horizontal plane as it comes forward, takes a slightly upward course as contact is made with the ball. This is the beginning of the follow-through, which brings the racquet and arm in line with the direction of the ball (Picture 6), and then across the body in an upward movement (Picture 7) that ends with the racquet head above and wide of the left shoulder (Picture 8).

With some players, the bevel or inclination increases on the follow-through until the racquet face is horizontal. This is characteristic of those who use the Western drive. I usually finish with the face about half way between the vertical and horizontal (Picture 8). If the ball is hit perfectly flat without over-spin, the racquet head moves in the same plane both before and after the moment of impact, and the face of the racquet remains practically vertical on the follow-through.

The flat drive has had a great deal of publicity in recent years, particularly since Ellsworth Vines got to the top with it, but, as a matter of fact, far fewer shots are hit flat than you might be led to believe. It is the Eastern drive rather than the flat drive that has become popular.

Very few players who use the Eastern grip hit the ball perfectly flat consistently. Some degree of spin is used on most shots, for the reason that it is difficult to control the ball without the spin. The confusion is to be attributed to the fact that the Western grip is commonly associated with the top-spin drive, and the Eastern forehand, on which less over-spin is generally used, is identified as the flat drive.

For the beginner and the intermediate player, I do not

recommend using the flat drive more than a quarter of the time, because of the greater risk attached. It is wonderfully effective as a put-away shot or to open the court for the volley, as Vines has demonstrated, but the margin of safety is so small, as compared with the over-spin drive, that it does not pay dividends if your timing or touch is the least bit off. It makes for more speed but also for more errors, and few players can afford the gamble of using it all the time. My advice is to apply at least a little over-spin most of the time. Additional speed is worthless without control.

There is the third type of drive in which, instead of coming over the ball to give it top-spin, you hit under it. The bevel is in the opposite direction, with the lower edge of the racquet forward. The undersliced shot is effective on turf, where it makes for a low, skidding bounce, but it is not easy to master and on surfaces where the balls get lighter it is particularly difficult to control. I would advise against the use of this drive, except as a variation to fall back upon in the effort to break up your opponent's game when your over-spin or flat stroke is not getting results.

The Backhand Drive

The principles that apply to the production of the forehand drive should be followed out in making the backhand drive on the other side of the body. Because the arm is carried across the body and there is not the natural freedom of movement in making the swing that there is on the right side, correct footwork and weight-shifting are even more important in the backhand than in the forehand drive, though they are never to be slighted in any stroke.

Unless you take the side stance properly, your backswing will be restricted, the elbow will be cramped against the body instead of being held well away from it, and the forward movement of the racquet will be impeded. Without the proper position, it will be impossible for you to bend your knee and put your weight behind the stroke; as a result, your timing, smoothness, and follow-through will suffer.

Your position in waiting for your opponent to make his shot is the same as in the forehand. You stand facing the net with your eyes on the ball (Picture 1). As the ball approaches, you turn—this time to the left, with the left foot going back and pointing towards the sideline—and the racquet head starts back (Pictures 2 and 3).

You will note how far around I turn for my backswing (Picture 4). My body has pivoted so far to the left that my back is half turned to the net as I watch the ball over my right shoulder. I am now in the position to pivot back to the right and carry the racquet forward well away from the body in a smooth, even stroke, and at the same time to transfer my weight naturally to the right foot (Picture 5).

The ball is hit approximately a foot ahead of the right hip (Picture 6). The shoulder and hip are held back until the impact, and at that instant the full weight is upon the right foot and the knee is bent. My posture as I hit the ball is not quite orthodox. I do not bend the right knee as much as correct form prescribes. I am more erect and hit almost from the perpendicular (Picture 6), unless I am taking a low ball.

After contact with the ball, the racquet head continues on up and across the body in the follow-through (Pictures 7 and 8). At the finish (Picture 8), it is slightly above

1

2

3

4

THE BACKHAND DRIVE
(Over)

Photographs by Harold McCracken

5

6

7

8

THE BACKHAND DRIVE
(Continued)

Photographs by Harold McCracken

and clearly wide of the right shoulder. The body swings back around to the right until you are almost back in the waiting position facing the net.

The racquet face is almost vertical and the wrist straight at the impact (Picture 6). There is a slight forward bevel of the top edge for the imparting of top-spin, as in the forehand. Just before the ball is struck, the racquet head, which is below the ball, takes a slightly upward course, marking the beginning of the follow-through, as in the forehand.

There is a tendency to underhit the backhand more than the forehand, by tilting the bottom edge of the racquet forward. While the undersliced drive is common and the spin it imparts is effective on grass in keeping the ball low, I favor the over-spin shot and hitting straight into the ball. The over-spin shot is easier to control, particularly in stroking a light ball, carries more power, and makes a better passing shot.

Remember that control is the first and most important consideration in your stroke production. It makes no difference how hard you hit the ball or how much "stuff" you put on it in the way of spin to unsettle your opponent's stroke unless you have accuracy and can keep it in the court. It is better to sacrifice something in speed and maintain control rather than try to kill every ball.

When you have mastered your strokes to the point where you can force without strain or losing control, that will be the time to adopt bolder measures. Until you have reached that stage, it will pay you to hit temperately with good length and concentrate on your timing and footwork.

Learn to take the ball on the rise, before it has reached the top of its bounce, and you will find that you will get extra speed with less effort. The pace on your opponent's ball is at the maximum just as it comes off the ground and, taken then, adds all the more to the speed of your own shot, without any straining. It is not easy to master the timing of taking a rising ball, but the dividends it pays make the effort worth while.

Remember to keep your eye glued on the ball. Take the correct side stance with the hip parallel to the net. Keep the racquet well away from the body so as not to cramp your stroke. Let your weight go forward with your racquet so that it is all on the front foot as you make contact in advance of the hip nearer the net. Bend the front knee to assist you in getting the body into the stroke, and let the racquet continue on up and across the body in a follow-through that will insure your getting the maximum control and pace.

All of this will come instinctively and mechanically if you get in the habit of doing it correctly. It's the best habit I know of for a tennis player.

5

The Spectacular: Serve and Smash

ONE OF THE MOST valuable of the tennis player's weapons is the service. It is the beginning of every point, and thus has an important bearing on who strikes the first strong blow, according to the effectiveness or weakness with which it is delivered. That does not necessarily mean that it will decide the outcome of the point, for a powerful service may be returned for a winner, and an ordinary one may sometimes be "flubbed" by the receiver and knocked astray. But in the majority of cases, a strong service, if it does not score outright, enables you to become the aggressor and force your opponent into a defensive return, and thus gives you the attacking position you need to administer the finishing thrust.

A first-class service is also a splendid ace in the hole. From my experience in any number of matches, I can tell you that it is a big comfort to have a "cannonball" serve at your command to help you through in a spot when the tide is going against you and your other weapons are unequal to pulling you out of the hole. How many, many times Tilden confounded his opponents when he seemed to be in trouble by suddenly letting loose a succession of lightning-like serves! Doeg, Vines, Shields, Stoefen and all the other players who had great services did the same thing. You may not have the physical strength, however, to bear down with it all through the match, and it is advisable to relax its pressure from time to time lest you expend so much energy on it that you weaken yourself and undermine the control of the rest of your game.

The mere knowledge on the part of your opponent that you have a big service may work to your advantage psychologically. Realizing how difficult it is to "break through" your service unless he is lucky, he is under a constant strain to win his own. He is always mindful of the fact that one loss of his own will probably cost him the set. The result is likely to be that he will put everything he has into winning his own service games and that he will not be able to threaten as much when he is receiving as he would against an opponent whose service did not keep him under such tension.

John Doeg's service, as we have observed, was decidedly a mental hazard for those who faced him. The rest of his game was less than first-class and he had to rely upon a chop for a forehand, but his terrifically fast delivery with its sharp break was such a dreaded scourge that he was able to defeat opponents who had the better stroke equipment and win the championship.

Recognizing the tremendous asset that the service can be, it is difficult to understand why so few players from other countries have come up with really good ones. Lacoste and Cochet had only fair ones when they won the Davis Cup for France and went ahead of Tilden. Borotra, whose attack was built around his service and volley, had a much stronger one, but it was not up to the best American standards.

Patterson of Australia was the only foreign player in the twenties who had a real cannonball. The Japanese were weak in service, although Kumagae, Shimizu and Harada played first-class tennis. The brilliant Alonso of Spain almost tied himself up in knots and stumbled over his feet in delivering the ball. The English services were gentle.

Of late years there has been a change in this situation. The value of the service has come to be recognized and more effort is being put into it by foreign players, although, with the exception of Quist, the Australians, who rank as the United States' most dangerous rivals for the Davis Cup, have not made much headway with it. Bromwich, their champion, hits the ball mildly and drops the second ball on the court (if the first is good) to get both hands on the racquet for his ambidextrous stroke production. Still, there are more good servers outside of the United States today than there were here in the entire decade from 1921 to 1930. Perry and Hare of England, Von Cramm and Henkel of Germany, Kukuljevic of Yugoslavia, Menzel of Sudeten Germany, Petra of France, and Quist are among the best.

The example furnished by Americans has undoubtedly been responsible for the foreign boom in services. The United States has had a constant succession of first-class servers, and the capital they have made of this weapon has opened the eyes of Europeans to their neglect. Their awakening was a long time in coming, for big serves were common in the United States twenty-five years ago.

McLoughlin, Williams, Murray and Voshell were hitting cannonballs in the years just prior to and after the war, and then came Tilden, who appeared to be able to serve an ace any time he needed a point in the hole. After Tilden there have been Shields, Wood, Doeg, Allison, Stoefen, Lott, Mangin, Bell, Eddie Jacobs, Dave Jones, Vines, Kovacs and Ballagh—all of them possessing fine services.

Possibly the explanation for so many good American services lies in the fact that the motion of delivering the service is the same as that which a baseball pitcher goes through in hurling the ball. Practically every tennis player has had his fling at baseball, and the experience should have benefited his service.

You take the same side stance for the service that you take in the pitcher's box. The same principles of footwork, body and arm action, and weight-shifting are carried out. Both the pitcher and the server go through a wind-up to gain momentum.

The Service

To take the proper position for the service, for which I use the Continental grip, place the left foot forward a few inches in back of the baseline. The right foot is from 12 to 18 inches behind the left, depending upon your height, and the right heel forms an angle of from 35 to 45 degrees with the left. Your body is sideways to the net with your left shoulder pointing towards the court into which you will serve (Picture 1). Your weight should be evenly balanced on your toes.

As you throw the ball up and start the backswing, your

THE SERVICE
(Over)

Photographs by Harold McCracken

5

6

7

8

THE SERVICE
(Continued)

Photographs by Harold McCracken

weight goes back to the right foot (Picture 2). In bringing the racquet up overhead in a circling motion continuous from the backswing, your weight is transferred to the left foot (Pictures 3 and 4), and as the racquet comes forward overhead you pull yourself up on your left toe to gain the maximum height at the moment of impact (Pictures 5 and 6).

In other words, the same principle of weight-shifting is carried out in both the serve and the drive, but a better analogy is furnished by the motion of a baseball pitcher. The whole force of the body is carried forward rhythmically along with the movement of the arm and is injected into the throw of the baseball or the swing of the racquet, both of which are made with the weight on the left toe.

After contact is made, the racquet comes down across the body in a follow-through (Picture 7), and your weight falls upon the right foot, which naturally comes to a position even with or just ahead of the left foot (Picture 8).

The toss of the ball for the service has an important bearing upon the success of the delivery and should be synchronized with the swing of the racquet. It must be thrown at the correct height so as not to delay or interfere with the completion of the swing, which should be smooth and continuous from the time you start to take the racquet back until the follow-through is completed.

Your object is to make impact at the top of the reach of your upstretched arm (Picture 6). If you throw the ball too high, the forward swing of your racquet from overhead must be delayed to permit of contact in the center of the face. The result is that you lose the effect of your preliminary swing and do not get the full weight of the body into the stroke, the momentum having been interrupted. The consequences are that the speed of the serve is reduced, and the accuracy of its placement may be marred by hitting the ball off center or on the wood at the top of the frame.

Failure to throw the ball high enough may work as great harm as tossing it too high. Instead of having to pause in your swing, you now must hurry it, at the sacrifice of rhythm, and you are unable to hit the ball at full height. This results in a cramped forward stroke, lowers the margin of clearance above the net, and thus makes it more difficult for you to reach your target. Another mistake is to toss the ball too wide, making it necessary for you to swing out to the side to bring the racquet against it. The weight of the body is thereby lost to the forward swing and the result is a jerky, badly sliced serve of reduced speed.

Experience and practice will enable you to master the trick of tossing the ball at the correct height and in proper timing for your swing. Proper height and rhythm permit your weight to go forward naturally in a continuous stroke.

Preparatory to starting the serve, my policy is to hold the ball and the racquet close together in front of the waist as I observe the position of the receiver (Picture 1). As I settle back, with a slight sway, to the right foot, I bring the left hand up with the toss and carry the racquet back and down at the full length of my right arm (Picture 2). The swing continues on without any hitch and with increasing momentum as I bring the racquet up to describe a partial loop behind the head, with the forearm bent back horizontally (Pictures 3 and 4).

The forearm now straightens out vertically (Picture 5), carrying the racquet the maximum distance above the head in the forward motion, which represents the peak of the swing's acceleration (Picture 6). The instant before contact is made with the ball, the left foot pivots slightly to the left from the toe—the reaction to the pull of the right arm. The change in the angle of the foot in this pivot can easily be observed (Pictures 3, 4, and 5).

As the ball is struck, the top of the racquet is inclined forward slightly (Picture 6). The degree of the tilt varies according to the height of the player. The taller he is, as a rule, the greater the inclination. The player of short stature does not have as great a margin of clearance over the net, and therefore hits the ball with the racquet held more nearly vertical. If your serves are going into the net, you may be tilting the racquet too much; and if they are reaching beyond the service line, the fault may lie in not enough tilt.

After the impact, the racquet continues on in the follow-through. It is highly important that its downward movement be directed in line with the spot towards which you are aiming the ball, and that the shoulder and arm be pointed in this same line (Picture 7). The stroke ends with the racquet coming down across the body to a position wide of and below the left knee (Picture 8), helping to preserve your balance for quick action on your next shot.

There are three types of service that are widely used. One is the flat service, another is the slice, and a third is the American twist. The fundamentals are the same for all three with respect to footwork, balance and weight-shifting. The differences lie in the angle of the racquet face as presented to the ball, and in the spin imparted. Some players, too, throw the ball up a little differently.

The flat service is made with the face of the racquet completely open. The ball is hit from behind and slightly above, making for the maximum speed. This is the fastest type of service and is the real "cannonball," though any fast service that goes for a winner is popularly called a cannonball. On grass and concrete the flat service is highly effective, but it loses some of its speed on clay, which slows down the ball. It is recommended for your first serve, but it is too risky to employ on your second ball. The margin of safety is too small. Also, its effect may be wasted against players who thrive on speed.

In the slice service, the racquet head comes around the outside of the ball and hits across towards the left as well as down, thus imparting side-spin. The ball does not leave the face of the racquet as quickly as it does on the flat serve. This results in a sacrifice of speed but makes for more control. It is a safer serve than the flat and its side-spin causes the ball to take a low bounce on grass, which is not likely to be relished by the receiver. You are less likely to make double faults if you use it for your second service than if you use the flat. One thing against the slice is that it makes the ball break to the receiver's forehand, usually his strong side, but it is possible to get so sharp a break as to defy a safe return.

Most players throw the ball up above their right shoulder for the flat and slice services. I advocate tossing it more to the left, because it forces you to sway slightly out after it and assists you to get your weight behind the ball. In making the American twist service, the toss is over the left shoulder (Pictures 2 and 3). The face of the racquet is brought sharply over the ball from left to right, applying top-spin that has the reverse effect from the side-spin of the slice. The ball takes a high bound and "kicks" sharply to the receiver's left, forcing him to take it on the backhand.

This is the type of service I have used from the start and I regard it as the best for beginners because of its safeness. You may find it a bit taxing to use it constantly, for it does not come quite as naturally as do the other two types. I had some difficulty with it at first. Like Joe Hunt, I developed a hitch, but I gradually ironed it out and now make it with a continuous motion.

Develop a Cannonball—Gradually

The bane of many players in the early stage of their development, and of some all through their career, is double faulting. This may result from being too daring with the second ball, or from trying to do too much with the first. Some hit with all their might on the first serve and merely tap the second over safely to invite murder. That is almost as bad as double faulting.

My advice is to work towards developing a serve of moderately good pace for both balls and to avoid the extremes of speed and weakness. I am not trying to discourage you from developing a cannonball. It is a great asset to have one, but I believe that you will get better results, particularly in the formative years of your game, if you concentrate on mastering a fairly stiff first serve and a second that is only a little less severe. Your first ball will go in much more frequently; and when it does not, you will not have to offer your opponent a setup on the second.

Use the flat or slice for your first ball and the slice or twist for your second, or, if you like the twist well enough, hit both serves with top-spin. Don't strain too much for the cannonball. It takes a lot out of you and every fault is only so much wasted energy. Concern yourself more with getting the ball in play with a forcing shot that will put the receiver under pressure and restrict his return. Mix up your pace and spin to keep him guessing and don't let him get set for the same kind of service every time.

Variation of the speed and spin of your serve will have beneficial results, and following it to the net from time to time is good policy. Some players make a practice of going up to volley behind every service. This is not the wisest procedure, in my opinion. It calls for too great a physical effort, in conjunction with what you put into the serve, to permit you to keep it up very long without slowing up your whole game and losing control.

Adopt the policy, rather, of going up occasionally and at unexpected moments to add to the element of surprise. It will increase the receiver's burden in returning your service because he will not know in advance where you will be. If you go up all the time, you give him a set target, and the same is true if you always stay back.

The matter of going in with the service to volley brings up the footfault. You can footfault whether or not you go to the net, but it is generally those players who rush to close quarters behind the service who violate the rule most often. At least, they are the ones who have footfaults called on them the most. They are the ones who benefit the most by the infraction, since it helps them to get into volleying position more quickly by starting ahead of the ball and lessens the chance of their being "passed" or caught in the wrong spot for their volley.

But whether or not you go to the net on your service, guard carefully and scrupulously against this distressing violation. Every game has its rules for the protection of both sides and to prevent either taking advantage of the other. Without these rules there wouldn't be any fun in playing or any satisfaction in winning, and a lot of bad feeling would result. It is to your interest to see that the rules are lived up to and enforced, and there is no other rule in the code that causes quite so much distress or to which more serious consideration should be given by the beginner than the footfault provision.

My match with Adrian Quist in the Davis Cup challenge round series with Australia at the Germantown Cricket Club in 1938 furnished a typical example of how footfaults can spoil the enjoyment of the play. The United States was leading by 2 matches to 1 when Quist and I went on the court in the first of the two final-day singles. Australia needed to win this one, or else it was beaten and its hopes of lifting the cup were ended.

We were in a very close first set with the score at 5-4 in my favor when the first of a number of footfaults was called on Adrian. The gallery immediately expressed its disapproval of the penalty, and when other footfaults followed, the spectators exploded so noisily in resentment that play had to be interrupted. The umpire pleaded with the crowd to remember that the game was played according to rules, explained that the captain of the Australian team acknowledged the footfaults had actually been made, and pointed out that the official who called them was only doing his duty.

The gallery still did not like it. I was certainly not happy about it. It is not pleasant to win points in a close match of such crucial importance, or in any match, on penalties, even though they are justified. The official on whom the crowd vented its displeasure couldn't have been very happy in performing a thankless task, and I am sure that Adrian was distressed, aside from the fact that he had lost a number of points.

From my associations with Quist as a friend and competitor, there is no question in my mind that there was no intent on his part to gain an unfair advantage by footfaulting. As a matter of fact, he was gaining no advantage at all. He was not following his service to the net, nor was he leaping into the air to hit the ball at a higher level.

His footfault was what might be called a technical one, although, nevertheless, it was a violation of the rule. It happened because he had not been able to correct an unfortunate habit of skipping forward on his left foot, and even though he moved back several feet behind the baseline to serve, he still could not eliminate the illegal motion. Adrian and all the other members of the Australian team took the penalties in the right spirit and with good sportsmanship, and I understand that he has made a very determined effort since he returned home to overcome this tendency.

The lesson in this is that every beginner in tennis should make up his mind to learn to serve without footfaulting. It calls for a real effort, as shown by the number of prominent players who have had footfaults called on them.

Frank Shields has been penalized time and again, and Sidney Wood had enough footfaults called on him in a Davis Cup match with Fred Perry at Wimbledon to have almost ruined his chances of winning. Frank and Sidney are among the finest sportsmen tennis has known. They simply were careless or were unable to correct a habit they had contracted in their early years. Unless you get in the habit of observing the rule while you are learning to serve, it may cause you no end of aggravation.

The rule says that throughout the delivery of the service you shall not change your position by walking or running, that you shall maintain contact with the ground and that you shall keep both feet behind the baseline. That means no leaping into the air with both feet off the ground, and no hopping or skipping. It means also that your right foot (or left foot if you serve left-handed with the right foot forward) shall not swing across the baseline before the moment of impact.

It is in this latter respect that most footfaults are made by the player who follows his service to the net. In his hurry to start forward, his rear foot swings across before the ball has been hit. He may be only a fraction of a second too hasty, but a competent, conscientious official will penalize him for it.

I don't want to set myself up as a model of virtue, but I have never had any difficulty with the footfault rule. My brother, Lloyd, taught me the importance of observing it as a junior, and the habit has stayed with me. If you will observe Picture 6 in the service series you will note that the left foot is clearly behind the line and that the right foot has not swung across at the moment of impact. Keep this picture in your mind when you serve. It may help to save you many points and possibly some matches.

But don't obey the rule just because it is to your advantage to do so. Do it in the spirit of fairness to your opponent and to those who have come to enjoy the match. That is the spirit in which lawn tennis was conceived and is played.

The Smash

The overhead smash is made with precisely the same stroke that is the service, and all the principles that apply to the latter should be carried out in the execution of this lethal shot, one of the most decisively hit in tennis. Instead of taking the ball in back of the baseline after tossing it up yourself, you deal with a ball that has been lofted over your head (lobbed) by your opponent to trap you as you rush to the net or to drive you back from the volleying position.

You smash the lob down from any position in the court between the net and the baseline, most often between the net and the service line. If the lob is an unusually good one and forces you to run back, you take it on a high rise after it has struck the ground in deep court and there are times occasionally when you smash it on the bounce from behind the baseline. But, generally speaking, the smash is to be identified as a service made around mid-court or closer up in answer to a ball thrown up by your opponent's racquet.

As a rule, a player who has a good service has a good smash, which is logical enough considering how much the two strokes have in common. There are the usual excep-

1

2

3

4

THE SMASH
(Over)

Photographs by Harold McCracken

5

6

7

8

THE SMASH
(Continued)

Photographs by Harold McCracken

tions. Tilden never was able to achieve the mastery of the smash that he had of everything else in the game. He never had quite the confidence to kill the ball as he did with his service and ground strokes.

Reversing the picture, Gene Mako, whose smashing I learned to appreciate and evaluate so highly while playing alongside him in the doubles court, has a comparatively mild service, though when he first came East it was hit much more strongly. Henri Cochet, too, killed the ball overhead with far more severity than he served.

To substantiate my original observation, there are the instances of Gerald Patterson and Quist of Australia, Gottfried von Cramm of Germany, Fred Perry of Great Britain, John Doeg, Lester Stoefen, Ellsworth Vines, Wilmer Allison, Frank Shields, Sidney Wood, Maurice McLoughlin, Howard Voshell, Richard Norris Williams, Lindley Murray, Gregory Mangin, Wayne Sabin, and Berkeley Bell. All of them had lethal services and all of them clouted their overheads.

The swing in making the overhead smash is so exactly the same as in serving that any detailed description would be only a repetition of earlier pages. Having dropped back to get under your opponent's lob (Pictures 1 and 2), you crouch slightly with a bend of the knees. The weight of the body rests upon the right or rear foot as the racquet starts back (Picture 3).

As the racquet comes around and makes a loop in back of the head, the body is lifted on the right foot (Pictures 4 and 5). The weight is transferred to the left foot as the arm straightens out and brings the racquet forward for the impact (Picture 6). The ball is hit at the top of the swing, and to strike it at the maximum height you pull yourself up on your left toe or leap into the air. After contact is made, the racquet continues on in the follow-through the same as in the service, with the right arm and shoulder in line with the direction of your smash (Picture 7). At the finish of the stroke, the racquet has crossed the body and is extended wide of the left knee (Picture 8).

The smash is made with either a flat or sliced service stroke. I prefer the flat type for the greater speed it imparts. However, the sliced overhead can be highly effective in putting the ball away because of the angle you get to pull the ball wide of the court.

The shorter your opponent's lob is, the more effectively you are able to deal with it because of the greater margin of clearance over the net. The deeper lobs are not so easy to kill and should be returned with a forcing smash that will enable you to get back to close quarters. In going back for a lob that catches you rushing in, I recommend that you turn and run to get under it rather than back up on your heels. The latter method is slower and you may lose your balance.

Whenever possible, make your smash without going off the ground for the ball. If you do jump, special pains must be taken to time your leap accurately. I have a tendency to go off the ground too soon and as a result sometimes hit the ball while I am coming down. Speed is lost through such mistiming, and the shot may go astray.

As much as possible, avoid letting the ball get behind you, else you will be forced to hit it in back of your head, and it is difficult to bring this kind of shot down into the court. If you misjudge the lob or are unable to get back under it to take it safely in the air, let it hit the ground, giving you time to run around in back of it, and take it on the bounce. Any unusually high lob of any depth is more safely to be dealt with by first letting it drop.

The success of your overhead will be determined not only by the timing and soundness of your stroke but also by your alertness and judgment while going to the net. The player who blindly rushes all the way in at top speed with the one fixed idea of volleying at close quarters may be running into a trap. He is inviting his opponent to throw the ball over his head; and if the lob has good depth and pitch, he will find it difficult to check his momentum enough to turn and scurry back in time to return it.

The effort to get as close to the net as possible for your volley is to be commended as increasing your chances of making a winning shot. However, it is one thing to go up with your eyes open and prepared for every contingency, and another thing to charge in impetuously without giving thought to the surprise that may be in store for you.

Don't let the fear of a lob discourage you from seeking the correct volleying position close in, but every time you go to the net be on your guard against it. Watch your opponent's racquet for an indication of the nature of his return. If he discloses the intent to lob, or the pressure of your approach shot allows him no other alternative, be prepared to fall back for a smash. So long as you are not taken completely by surprise you will be able to get under his toss. In other words, keep your wits about you and you will make it easier for yourself; that applies whether you are smashing, volleying, or making any other stroke in tennis.

The Volley

*T*HE WINNING GAME in tennis today is played both in the vicinity of the baseline and inside the service court. It is the game of the drive and the volley. It is a game built upon the sound foundation of strong ground strokes and reared to full stature on the authority of your command of the net.

The drive must necessarily be the prime factor of any successful game, but, without its volleying adjunct, the full profit of its strength cannot be reaped. Power is wasted, openings for finishing thrusts are sacrificed, and the verdict is needlessly deferred at the expense of energy you may need for the next match.

The methods of the players who have won the championship during the past decade emphasize how much of a factor the volley has become in top-notch tennis. Since William Tilden last held the crown in 1929, every wearer of the purple has established his supremacy with the help of his net attack.

John Doeg, Ellsworth Vines, Fred Perry and Wilmer Allison all have used the volley at every opportunity. In women's tennis, too, it has been the same story. Miss Helen Jacobs and Miss Alice Marble, who have won the title between them in six out of the last seven years, both have excelled in the forecourt, and Miss Marble, the present champion, is one of the finest volleyers in the history of women's tennis.

Most beginners are slow to take up the volley. In a way, that is a good thing, for it is important that they first equip themselves with competent ground strokes. After they have become trained in the fundamentals, accustomed their eyes to the flight of the ball, and developed their sense of timing, it is time for them to learn to take the ball in its flight up forward.

Many continue to be backward about leaving the baseline no matter how long they have been playing, and some of them never get up the courage to go to the net. The thought of meeting the ball "head on" at close range, so to speak, is too much for them. They lack confidence in themselves and they have the idea that it is beyond the capacity of any save the exceptional player to learn to volley well.

I can remember how timid I was about going to the net. There was a time when I liked my baseline so much that I practically had to get a personal invitation from my opponent in the form of a shot that struck in the forecourt to unanchor myself. I had to learn to come up and like it. It wasn't until 1935, when I made my first trip to Wimbledon, that it dawned on me how big a factor the volley is in tennis and how much the progress of my game had been held up by my neglect of this phase of the attack.

Seeing Perry in action opened my eyes. The quickness with which he could get in to the net and finish off the points, instead of staying back and pumping away in long rallies, convinced me of the error of my ways. This was the way the world's greatest amateur played tennis and I became completely sold on it, so much so that I went home and worked so hard on my volley that in the final of the 1936 championship at Forest Hills I was rushing the net even more than Fred was.

Hit and Run—To the Net

The volley is an important stroke because of the pressure it puts on your opponent to extract an error from him if it does not score a clean winner, and because of the energy it saves you in bringing the rallies to an early conclusion. Against a baseline player of the steadiness of Bryan Grant, who can retrieve any except the fastest putaway drives, it is particularly helpful to have a net attack.

To stay back and trade drives with a player of this type can be very discouraging, if not downright annoying. The ball keeps coming back until you make up your mind to gamble on the smallest possible margin of safety to break through his defense. The volley simplifies your problem because it enables you to capitalize immediately a forcing drive whose advantage to you may be lost by your failure to follow it in.

There is a certain amount of risk in going to the net; but if you are a good volleyer and have the proper ground strokes to provide reasonably safe approach, there is even more risk for your opponent. Stationed at the center of the net, which should be your position except at times when your drive has forced your opponent so wide as to close off a part of your court to his return, you are able to cover all but a foot or two of your territory on either side. The result is that he often tries for the opening down the sidelines and makes an error.

When your approach shot has forced him wide, you cover more to that side because the angle from which he is hitting restricts his target on the other side of your court to a segment. But whether you hit down the middle or to the corner, the pressure is on your opponent and often causes him to hurry his return, to take his eye off the ball in watching you, or to gamble on a passing shot, all of which are conducive to errors.

The risk for you in going to the net lies in your approach at the wrong time on a weak drive, in your failure to go in fast enough, or in your being trapped by a lob. Your approach shot must have good depth and pace to force your opponent and prevent him from knocking the ball back past you before you have reached a volleying position.

Don't go in on a drive you hit from behind your baseline. Preferably, wait for your opponent to give you a short ball. If he is hitting consistently deep, you must make your own opportunity by taking the ball on the rise and starting forward instantly. Once you have headed for the net, get in swiftly all the way or else you will be caught too far back and have to make a difficult volley close to the ground, or a half volley.

Fear of the other fellow's lob should not keep you from getting in close enough. So long as you keep your eyes open and are prepared to check your momentum the instant he discloses the intent to throw the ball over your head, you will have time enough to get back under it unless he is exceptionally clever in concealing his stroke and gets just the necessary height and pitch on the ball. The player who is on his toes mentally as well as literally is in no great danger of being trapped.

To come to the technique of the volley, we start with the grip. The same three types of grip that I have previously discussed are used for the volley. Personally, I am partial to the Eastern. The Western is unsuitable for a low volley and there is a tendency to hit under the ball and apply too much back-spin with the Continental.

The Western is used very successfully by some players on volleys above the top of the net. With the wrist directly behind the handle, you can get a tremendous amount of punch into your volley, and the more speed, the more effective the shot. William Johnston, one of the greatest volleyers the game has seen, used the Western grip, and Wilmer Allison, one of the finest in recent years, advocates it along with the Eastern. Gregory Mangin murdered high balls with the Western.

The effectiveness of the Western in taking a high ball stands out all the more in contrast with the Continental. With the Continental it is almost impossible to make a smashing volley at shoulder height. On the other hand, the Western is just as unsuitable for making a low volley unless you crouch down to the ball. The Continental is adapted to taking a low volley, or a rising ball with a half volley. Fred Perry gets a lot of touch into these shots with the Continental, and, of course, speed does not enter greatly into any stroke made up close to and below the level of the net.

While the Western and the Continental both have their strong points and may be superior for certain shots, for all-round effectiveness I prefer the Eastern. Some players use more than one grip, but I find that the Eastern is serviceable for all volleys, regardless of the level at which they are made. Furthermore, I think it is better to stick

1

2

3

4

THE FOREHAND VOLLEY
(Over)

Photographs by Harold McCracken

5

6

7

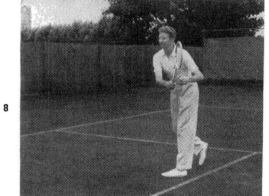

8

THE FOREHAND VOLLEY
(Continued)

Photographs by Harold McCracken

to one grip. Vincent Richards, a really great volleyer, used the Eastern.

Forehand and Backhand Volleys

In preparing to receive the ball for your volley, take a stance facing the net. In this position, you are prepared to move either to the right or left, according to whether it is to be a forehand or backhand volley (Pictures 1 and 1A). The weight of the body goes into the making of the volley as it does in the drive; you make a side turn to facilitate the transfer of your weight forward (Pictures 2 and 2A). In going to the net you do not have the time to set yourself for the stroke that you do in taking the ball on the bounce in the backcourt, and it is often necessary to volley while you are facing the net squarely. But, regardless of the stance from which you hit, you should get your weight behind the shot.

As the ball approaches, you make your backswing. It is not the long backswing that you use for the drive, and it does not, as a rule, go back much farther than the rear shoulder (Pictures 3 and 4, 3A and 4A). The length of your backswing will depend upon the type of volley you are making.

If you take the ball below the level of and close to the net with a lift volley, or if you simply block it, the backswing is almost negligible, and there is little follow-through. When you take the ball above the level of the net, you have a chance to get more punch into your shot, the backswing is longer (Picture 4A), and there is more follow-through in your stroke (Pictures 7A and 8A).

On shoulder-high shots at the net, the ball can be killed

with the so-called kill-volley or drive-volley. My back-swing on the kill-volley is started with the same loop that I make on my forehand drive. Instead, however, of bringing the racquet forward in line with the ball, I bring it forward and down on the ball from the height of the loop. The impact is made with an open-faced racquet, and the ball is hit flat with a force that generates so much speed as to permit of little chance of its being returned.

This stroke has gained a considerable vogue of late, and, in my opinion, has decided possibilities of adding to the effectiveness of the volleying attack. The French used it more than ten years ago. Jean Borotra used it on the backhand with the same motion with which he made his backhand drive. Jacques Brugnon hit it on the forehand. But the French had few imitators, though William Tilden and Sidney Wood at times have used almost a full swing on volleys above the net without getting the punch into the stroke that Borotra did.

Of recent years, Ellsworth Vines, Wilmer Allison, and Gene Mako have revived the drive-volley. Mako was the first one I saw make it, and he helped me master it. I feel that it has added a good deal to the strength of my net attack.

Returning to the standard volley, whether you use the long backswing or a shorter one, the ball should be met well in front of you if possible (Pictures 6 and 5A), and also as high as possible. The farther in front of you it is hit, the better chance you have to angle it, and the height enables you to hit down on the ball. The down-shot is the winner in tennis. There is less chance of the ball going into the net or overreaching the lines. Therefore, you can take greater liberties and kill it.

1A

2A

3A

4A

THE BACKHAND VOLLEY
(Over)

Photographs by Harold McCracken

5A

6A

7A

8A

THE BACKHAND VOLLEY
(Continued)

Photographs by Harold McCracken

The head of the racquet should always be above the level of the wrist in volleying (Pictures 3, 4, and 5; 3A, 4A, and 5A), except, of course, when you are taking a very low ball. You can keep it above the wrist on some of the low ones by stooping down to the ball.

The wrist is bent slightly as the racquet is carried back (Picture 4), but it straightens out in alignment with the arm as the racquet is brought against the ball. It is locked stiff at the moment of contact (Pictures 6 and 5A), thus bracing the racquet against the impact of the ball taken in full flight. More speed is thereby picked up by your volley from your opponent's ball with this rigid resistance, whereas if the wrist were loose and relaxed, your racquet might be deflected by a hard-driven shot and your ball would fail to accumulate this increment of speed. Additional punch is supplied to your volley by the action of the forearm and the reinforcement of the shoulder.

The majority of volleys are hit either flat or with a slight under-spin. On volleys taken above the level of the net, a little over-spin can be used, though some players are opposed to this. I prefer to hit the ball flat, using a forward bevel of the bottom edge of the racquet (Picture 6) to give lift to the ball on low volleys and of the upper edge for those made above the level of the net.

Under-spin slows up the speed of your shot, and there is a tendency to overhit the line with it, but is is useful on the lower volleys. Because the strings of the racquet are in contact with the ball longer, the undercut volley is better controlled, and the action of the spin on grass keeps the ball low.

The success of your volley will rest in large part upon what you do with the ball. As a general rule, the most successful volley is the one that is hit deep and with good pace. Some advocate hitting it deep down the middle rather than to the side, because there is less danger of your opponent passing you from the middle than there is if you gave him an angle on his return.

Vincent Richards almost never gave Tilden a wide ball on his backhand whether he (Richards) was hitting his approach shot or his volley. He found that Tilden passed his man in nearly every instance where he was given an angle on his backhand. Naturally, you have to make allowances and corrections for your opponent's specialties, but my contention is that so long as you have the necessary length and punch, your volley is likely to win for you regardless of whether or not you direct it down the center.

Seek for depth and pace rather than risky angles and drop volleys, which are made with a short chop stroke to fall just over the net and take a low sliding bounce because of the back-spin applied. Short, angled volleys and drop volleys are effective only if your opponent is so far to the other side of the court or so far back that he will not have the time to reach them, or if he is slow on his feet. Some players, Gene Mako among them, are successful with the drop volley and the short, angled variety, but many of these shots, falling a little too deep or anticipated by the opponent, can be returned for winners when a forceful volley to the baseline would have beaten him or at least permitted him to do little more than get the ball back.

The drop volley, made with the face of the racquet inclined back slightly to impart back-spin, and with very little follow-through to the short, chopping stroke, is recommended chiefly for close-up shots below the level of the net. Any time you get a ball above the net that permits you to hit down, lay into it and do not gamble with short angles or drops. These are useful as variations on the net-high volleys, and, interpolated occasionally as a surprise device, serve to catch your opponent unprepared too far back, but length and pace pay the big dividends with the volley as they do with the drive.

7

Auxiliary Strokes

THUS FAR, THESE pages have been devoted to a consideration of the fundamental or standard strokes of tennis, the
basic weapons indispensable for the development of a winning game. The player who masters or is reasonably
proficient in the execution of the drive, the service, the volley, and the smash has all the mechanical equipment necessary to go out on the court and give a very creditable account of himself. Championships have been won by men
and women who had nothing in addition, and, in some instances, less than the command of all four.

Nevertheless, as adequate as these instruments are to
meet the requirements of tournament competition, at the
same time there are others of secondary importance which
may be found very useful; some of them, indeed, have been
big factors in the success of players of wide reputation.
These strokes might be called auxiliary or subordinate
shots—accessories to the equipment of the completely
"turned out" tennis player. Added to the sound foundation of the standard strokes, they augment his feeling of
confidence and security because of his preparedness to re-
spond to the most exacting demands upon his repertory.
As the fellows say, he has all the answers.

Chiefly defensive measures, these auxiliaries, ready to

1

2

3

4

THE FOREHAND HALF VOLLEY
(Over)

Photographs by Harold McCracken

5

6

7

8

THE FOREHAND HALF VOLLEY
(Continued)

Photographs by Harold McCracken

come to your assistance in the emergency or when the pressure is on and your big guns are losing the fight, are the half volley, the lob, the chop, and the drop shot. All of them have offensive possibilities. Certainly, the half volley, as executed by a specialist, can be more dazzling and electrifying than any other shot in the game; but basically, they are defensive shots designed to extricate you from faulty positions, checkmate the attack of your opponent, or stem the tide when your standard strokes are not getting results, although in doubles the lob is classified differently.

I practically never have recourse to a regulation full-length chop stroke, nor do I have any great affinity for the lob in singles, and there are others of whom the same may be said. These strokes are, however, in the game, and they do serve a purpose; for some players, a very important purpose. So you should know them and cultivate two or three, if not all, of them. They will never do the rest of your game any harm, so long as you do not concentrate on them to the neglect of the basic strokes. Also, with the exception of the half volley, they do not call for any particularly difficult refinements of execution.

The principles that are carried out as to stance, footwork, and weight-shifting in making the standard shots apply to the auxiliaries, and once you have become schooled in the fundamentals you have only to master the technique of the stroke itself to add them to your equipment. Since the chop and drop shot are made with the same stroke, and the lob and the half volley are patterned after the drive, you do not have a great deal of new ground to cover.

The Half Volley

The half volley is the most misnamed shot in tennis. Actually, there is nothing of the volley about it, for the ball is hit after it has struck the court. In truth, it is a ground stroke on which the ball is taken at the earliest possible moment after its contact with the surface (Picture 5). It is comparable to the pick-up in baseball or the drop-kick in football and is generally an emergency measure.

The same principles apply for the half volley when it is made in back of the service line that are followed in the execution of the drive, forehand or backhand. As will be observed from the backhand illustration (Picture 2A), you take the same side stance, and there is the same shifting of the weight forward with the stroke from the rear foot when possible. The stroke is usually shorter than it is for the full-length drive, both as to the extent of the backswing and the follow-through, but there are some players who attack with the half volley from deep court with the same sweeping movement of the arm and racquet with which they drive.

The length of the backswing and follow-through is largely determined by your distance from the net and also by the amount of time you have to bring it off. The closer to the net you are, the shorter the stroke; and in the case of a net-rusher who is called upon to crouch quickly while in stride and take a fast-dropping ball at his feet, there may be little or no backswing. He drops his racquet on edge to the ground instantly, directly in back of where the ball strikes.

1A

2A

3A

4A

THE BACKHAND HALF VOLLEY
(Over)

Photographs by Harold McCracken

5A

6A

7A

8A

THE BACKHAND HALF VOLLEY
(Continued)

Photographs by Harold McCracken

The face of the racquet meets the ball almost flat (Picture 5). Since the ball has just started to rise as it is struck, it is necessary to check this impulse or your shot will be lofted into the air. This is accomplished by a slight forward beveling of the upper edge of the racquet, inclining the face towards the ground. The nearer to the net the half volley is made, the more careful you have to be about this bevel, as you may smother the ball and prevent it from clearing the net. On a real close-up shot, the bevel is in the opposite direction, with the face turned slightly upward, to give the necessary loft to clear the net.

From any point behind the service line, the half volley can be a brilliant attacking stroke, whereas close in it is almost entirely an emergency, defensive measure, although some players with a gifted touch and sense of timing can bring off perfectly stunning winners inside the service court. Farther back, it is taken with a forward-beveled racquet and a long backswing (Picture 4) and follow-through.

Richard Norris Williams, Henri Cochet and Vincent Richards excelled at this, and their half volley was premeditated and one of their most feared weapons. Williams and Cochet used it so much because they made a practice of taking a rising ball and regularly stood inside the baseline, where most players would be out of position and lost. Richards, who was always seeking to get to close quarters, used it to assist him in reaching the volleying position by successive stages when he could not go all the way in with a single stroke.

In the hands of marvelously adept players such as these and Gregory Mangin, whose close-up half volleys were breath-taking and seemingly miraculous, the shot could be strikingly successful; but even they missed their share, and for the player without their quick eye, reflex action, and rare sense of timing, the half volley is too risky to be used more than sparingly.

Taking the ball on the rise in backcourt with a regulation drive is quite a trick in itself, but the half volley goes considerably beyond that, and my advice would be to avoid it unless it is forced upon you when caught out of position; then necessity compels its use as an emergency stroke. Safer and more orthodox methods will pay greater dividends, and only the more advanced player with a delicate feel for the ball on the racquet should consider it as standard equipment for singles. In doubles, because the server is frequently forced to take the ball at his feet in joining his partner at the net, it is a different story, as will be told in a later chapter.

The Lob

The lob is the drive made with a mild impact and a slight, deliberate uplift of the racquet head constituting the follow-through. Instead of projecting the ball swiftly in a horizontal plane, you loft it into the air. Your purpose is to return it safely above the reach of your opponent, stationed or advancing to the net; or to allow yourself time to recover position or to slow up his attack and gain a breathing spell.

When executed in the approved manner, the shot starts and looks exactly like the drive, except that the backswing need not be quite as long. Its success is predicted in part upon this similarity, because it serves to disguise your purpose and makes for the element of surprise that is so essential. The racquet head is brought forward vertically in line with the ball and at moderate speed. The weight is transferred to the front foot, and, so far as your opponent can tell, the stroke will be just another drive. But, an instant before the impact, the swing is slowed down the slightest bit and, as the ball is struck, the racquet, instead of taking the usual course of the follow-through, is brought upward.

The face of the racquet strikes in back of the ball and comes slightly under it to impart under-spin for one type of lob. For the top-spin lob, the face comes over the ball on the lifting follow-through. Do not merely hit under the ball with the face inclined back from the vertical to the horizontal. The result of such a stroke is that the ball is tossed almost straight up and is easily dealt with by your opponent. Also, made in this way, its nature is immediately disclosed instead of remaining veiled almost to the moment of contact.

The most successful lob against the volleyer is the one that gives him no inkling of your purpose until he has committed himself to a position at the net. It has just enough height to escape his upstretched racquet, sufficient depth to make him scramble back quickly, and a forward pitch after striking the ground that carries it still farther away from him. The top-spin lob best achieves all this and as used by George Lott, one of the most accomplished lobbers in history, it is a feared instrument of attack rather than the usual defensive measure. George conceals the shot cleverly, keeps the trajectory down to almost the minimum level commensurate with safety, generally places it where his opponent least relishes it, which is over and beyond his left shoulder, and gets a pitch from the ground that defies recovery.

The top-spin lob can be concealed a little better than can the undercut. It comes down faster because of the action of the spin, and, as has been noted, it bounces forward in the direction of its flight, instead of straight up as does the under-spin lob.

If your purpose in lobbing is to regain position or catch your breath, you toss the ball higher and the under-spin shot serves nicely as the ball stays in the air longer. This is purely a defensive stroke and is more likely to be dealt with successfully by your opponent because of the additional time he has to prepare for it, whereas the top-spin lob offers a real possibility of scoring a winner.

However, one should use the lob sparingly in singles. Unless the opponent is taken by surprise at the net or is palpably weak in smashing overhead, anything less than a perfect toss is apt to meet with a painful reception. If your opponent is so good a volleyer that you cannot pass him, or if you are under pressure and need time to get into position or require a few moments' respite, the lob may help you; but offensively it does not serve you profitably enough to be used more than occasionally, except against a tactless net-rusher, who may be trapped or run to the point of exhaustion.

In doubles, it is a different story and the lob is one of the most effective strokes. Command of the net determines the outcome of most rallies; and the lob is often the salvation of the side that is receiving service, enabling it to dislodge the opponents and wrest the attack from them, if not to break up their formation and disrupt their teamwork.

Sidney Wood illustrates the position of the racquet at the moment of contact
in making a forehand lob.

Sidney Wood illustrates the position of the racquet at the moment of contact
in making a forehand chop.

The lob-volley, a lob made on the volley when both teams are at the net, accomplishes this in a spectacular way, taking the opponents completely unaware and driving them back frantically.

Consideration of the importance of the lob in the four-handed game will be given at more length in the pages devoted to doubles.

The Chop

Broadly speaking, the chop may be said to be the drive made with a chopping motion that imparts a different kind of spin to the ball. Some players have put so much stress upon it as to give it the status of a primary stroke. Beals Wright, national champion in 1905; Wallace Johnson, finalist in 1921; John Doeg, champion in 1930; George Lott, great in doubles and outstanding also in singles; Howard Kinsey, a former doubles champion; Berkeley Bell, former intercollegiate champion, and Bryan Grant and Frank Parker, both high ranking players, are among the men who have made big capital of the chop. Wilmer Allison, champion in 1935, added it to his repertory after his fame had been established, and has a particularly good one.

Miss Helen Jacobs, winner repeatedly of the championship, Miss Elizabeth Ryan, doubles champion on several occasions at Wimbledon and singles finalist at Forest Hills in 1926, and Baroness Maud Levi (now Mrs. Walter Blumenthal) have demonstrated that the women can use the chop proficiently too. Baroness Levi and Johnson chopped almost every ball they hit, including their service, ground strokes, and volleys.

The grip for the chop is half way between the Eastern forehand and backhand for both sides. The backswing is shorter than that for the drive. The racquet head, held above the level of the wrist, is brought back about even with the right shoulder and then forward and down from that height with a chopping motion. The shoulder leans into the ball and the weight is transferred to the left foot at the impact. The stroke is made decisively, with the wrist, arm and shoulder all contributing to its emphatic bite. The follow-through brings the racquet slightly below the left hip.

The face of the racquet is inclined backward as it is brought forward to strike in back of and under the ball. Back-spin is thus imparted to the ball, which causes it to rise in its flight but to take a low, shooting bounce. On a wet turf court, this bounce can be almost vicious as the ball skids from the surface.

The fact that the chop rises in crossing the net makes it a poor stroke to use against the volleyer, who is thus given the opportunity to hit down. The back-spin not only gives lift to the ball but also reduces its speed because of the fact that it is rotating backward and pulling against its forward flight. Thus, the volleyer has not only a high ball but a comparatively slow one as a target, whereas a top-spin drive, rotating forward, falls fast once it crosses the net, and compels him to volley up against more pace. Because of this reduction in speed and the generally higher trajectory, the chop is not as good a put-away shot as the flat or slightly topped drive against a baseliner, who has more time to return it.

On the other hand, the chop can be very effective in

breaking up the game or slowing down the attack of an opponent with a superior drive, particularly when it is used in conjunction with the drive. The change in spin and speed may unsettle his stroke, and, if he uses a Western grip, unsuited to taking a low ball, or likes the ball to come to him high, the low, sliding pitch of the chop from the ground may work havoc with his timing and balance. This is especially the case on a wet grass court.

Thus, a player with a particularly good chop, such as Bell's, may completely change the pattern of the play. If he does not disrupt his opponent's control, at least he may slow down the pace of the match, to give himself more time to get to the ball. Not only is his own shot slower, but, because of this, his opponent has to make his own pace.

As an approach shot to gain the net, the chop can be highly effective, as I learned in playing Bell at Longwood my first year East. Bell has given most of the ranking players trouble in stopping his net attack. His chop to the backhand keeps so low a trajectory and is hit so viciously and deep that it is exceedingly difficult to pass him.

It should be clear, then, that the chop has considerable to recommend it, although it almost never can take the place of a good drive. The chop has definite shortcomings and weaknesses, and anyone would be ill advised to concentrate on it at the expense of the other. The fact that so few players have been able to reach the top without the drive should be evidence enough of that. In general, as a defensive device to exploit weaknesses in your opponent's game and take him by surprise, or as a variation to slow up an attack that is too fast for you, the chop can be very useful on grass or dirt courts. On hard surfaces, its value diminishes because of the fact that the spin does not take effect.

The Drop Shot

The drop shot might be called the baby chop. It is the same stroke, except that it calls for less physical effort, a delicate rather than a vehement address to the ball, and a shorter follow-through. It is hit in this manner so that the ball, instead of being directed with sting into deep court, is dropped short just over the net to trap the other fellow off guard or too far back.

One of the riskiest of all shots, the drop must be played carefully and accurately; its success depends so much upon the opponent being taken by surprise that it is as likely to result disastrously as it is to win. If the opponent is prepared for it, or if the ball is played even a foot or two too deep, he runs in for an easy put-away shot.

Even when it is executed perfectly and the opponent is in deep court, it may fail. The ball, with back-spin and comparatively high trajectory, floats slowly through the air and takes a higher bound than does the viciously cut chop of full length, enabling the opponent to reach it in time.

Regardless of anything the opponent can do about it, the drop shot may very well result in the loss of the point. Because of the fact that it must necessarily be played so shallow, to defy recovery, the ball frequently fails to clear the net. It calls for the closest kind of gauging and sensitive "feel" to execute it with just the right length.

And yet, despite the riskiness of the shot, the drop has

had a big vogue of late. Although Miss Elizabeth Ryan used it with a high degree of success when she ranked among the best, it is only in recent years that it has really caught on and been taken up by most of the leading players. Robert Riggs is one of its most feared exponents and George Lott is another. Gene Mako, Bryan Grant, Frank Parker, Joe Hunt, Gilbert Hunt, and J. Gilbert Hall use it readily, and Miss Alice Marble, Mme. Sylvia Henrotin of France, and Señorita Anita Lizana of Chile (now Mrs. Roland Ellis of England) have good command of it. Mme. Henrotin's opponents have a dread of her drop, and Señorita Lizana made the day miserable for Mlle. Jadwiga Jedrzejowska of Poland using it in the final of our championship in 1937.

In the hands of a player who has the touch for it, the drop can be almost demoralizing for the opponent. Used in conjunction with the lob, it can inflict severe punishment, keeping him on the run between the net and the baseline. Some use it chiefly for this purpose of wearing down the opponent, considering the effort worth while even if the point is lost frequently.

On a day of excessive heat, the player who is repeatedly called on to rush up the court to retrieve a drop is likely soon to begin to droop and lose some of his control and speed. A player who finds himself far behind in the set may play drop after drop solely with the intent of reducing his opponent's strength for the next set.

It is good policy to employ the drop when you find yourself unable to penetrate your opponent's defense with your drive or get to the net. If he is slower in running up and back than he is across the baseline, or if he is none too secure in his volleying, the drop shot is likely to beat him or, if returned across court, it paves the way for a passing shot through the big opening straight down.

Some players resent their opponent's using the drop shot, or the "dink" shot as they scornfully refer to it. They appear to believe that there is something unsporting about it and that it is pat ball, not tennis. They are simply burying their heads in the sand and failing to realize that the game progresses.

There were people who felt the same way about the volley. The man who stood back and drove the ball deeper and faster and with better control than his opponent was the real tennis player. They said the volleyer was an upstart, with revolutionary ideas foreign to the traditions of a noble game, who should be escorted from the premises—and none too gently.

The drop shot is the newest development in tennis and, whether it is pat ball or not, it calls for the highest degree of skill in its delicate execution, and the exercise of discrimination and quick thinking in its interpolation at the right time. The risk attached to it is answer enough as to whether it is pat ball. For the untutored, its penalties are so severe that it might better be called pure dynamite—to be handled with care.

8

Psychology and Strategy

LAWN TENNIS IS the perfect game to play and watch because of the fact that it is so complete an all-round test. It is a game not only of the hand and foot, but, just as much, of the head and heart. The mental faculties are brought into play equally with the physical attributes, and a game of championship quality is evolved only through the proper functioning of both. Without the moral fiber, or heart, to persevere and carry on tenaciously in the face of the discouragement and adversity that are the lot of every player on the way to the top, not even the combination of outstanding mental and physical equipment will avail to get him there.

The casual layman who happens to attend a tournament to see the celebrities he has been reading about in the papers can scarcely have any conception of the battle of wits that is going on before his eyes. He sees two well set up young men or graceful young women hammering away at the ball, and he nods his head approvingly in appreciation of their quickness, their physiques, and the explosiveness of their shots.

Perhaps he admires the neatness with which one of them traps the other with a well-placed ball that can not be reached, or the agility with which one makes an almost miraculous recovery. Even if he knows little or nothing about the game, he can enjoy the spectacle, for tennis is so seemingly obvious in its fundamentals, as compared to, say, football that the spectator quickly gets the idea of the game. Yet, what he sees is only on the surface. The fine points of strategy and stroke production are often lost upon him, and it is these that decide most matches between players of comparatively equal ability.

Tennis strategy is divided into two phases. One has to do with the utilizing of your own strokes to the best advantage to overcome your opponent's defense. This is accomplished through the judicious selection of the right shot to meet each situation and to exact openings through the accumulative effect of your sequence of strokes. It is the strategy of the field general who skillfully directs his forces on the attack to expose a vulnerable point in the enemy's terrain.

The other phase concerns itself with the analysis of the opponent's game to ferret out weaknesses therein, and the adoption of measures calculated to be most effective in exploiting his failings or shortcomings. In the first instance, the effect of the strategy is positive in that your design is to vanquish your opponent through the superior strength and direction of your attack. In the second instance, it is negative; your purpose is not to build up, but to break down or undermine your opponent's weapons so that he will not be able to utilize them to the best advantage.

Rene Lacoste was noted for the emphasis he placed upon this second phase. He kept a book in which were catalogued the weaknesses of the players he had met, as revealed by his own observations and experiences, and also of those whom he might possibly have to meet, as reported to him by others.

If a player did not like a low slice to his backhand, or a chop to his forehand; if he hit more effectively on the run than while stationary, or vice versa; if he always hit across court from a certain position, rather than alternating at times to the shot straight down; if he was weak overhead or was susceptible to being trapped by a lob in his impetuous rush to the net; if he was slow of foot; if he had tendencies to stand too far back and take the ball late, or to stand in close and take it on the rise—all these weak points, strong points, and characteristics were in Lacoste's book. When he met the player, he went on the court prepared to attack his weaknesses and furnish an antidote to his strong measures, and so shrewd and analytical a mind was Lacoste's that nothing escaped him.

An analogy is furnished in the scouting system of football, except that in football it is not the players but the coaches who make the analysis. The football scout looks for weak points in the future opponent's defense, and attacking plays that might be unusually difficult to stop. He looks for tip-offs comparable to the tennis player's regularity in hitting across court from a certain position, and he finds them in the hitch that the halfback gives to his pants when he is to carry the ball or the end's change of stance when he is to go down for a pass.

I think that this analysis of your opponent's game can be carried too far in that you may neglect the development of your own offensive weapons and plan of attack in concentrating on the other man's weaknesses, though Lacoste never made this mistake. My own policy is that a strong offense is the best defense. It gives you more confidence to feel that your weapons are strong enough to win, regardless of what the other man does. I think there is more satisfaction, too, in winning through the merits of your own game rather than your opponent's defects.

However, I don't want to create the impression that the man who plays to his opponent's weaknesses is doing anything the least bit unsporting or that winning by this method is any less of an achievement. On the contrary, to go out against someone who is supposed to be your superior and defeat him through the intelligence of your tactics merits the highest praise.

Back in 1930, Ellsworth Vines came East for the first time and he was an immediate sensation. His terrific hitting power was too much for Frank Hunter and Frank Shields in two successive tournaments, and he was hailed as another California Comet, destined to rank with Maurice McLoughlin. Sidney Wood came through to the final at Seabright with Ellsworth, and practically everyone thought that Wood would be lucky to get a set. But Sidney didn't think so. He had analyzed Vines' game during the week and he confided to friends on the eve of the final that he had the answer to it. They thought he was having his joke; Vines would blow him off the court.

The next day Sidney gave Ellsworth one of the worst lickings of his life. He slow-balled him with soft, spin shots that ruined Vines' control. A lot of people in the gallery thought that it was a terrible match and they didn't feel so kindly towards Wood for spoiling their pleasure after they had come so far to see the final. They should have congratulated Sidney for a smart piece of head work. Vines, who was only a kid at the time, profited by that lesson. He told me later that he went home and worked all that autumn and winter in handling soft, spin shots. For eliminating this weakness from his game, he became all the greater a player, winning the championship in 1931.

Every player should acquaint himself with the different varities of spin and have them at his beck when needed for the purpose of variation. Personally, I depend upon controlled speed and do not mix my spin much with my ground strokes, never using a slice and seldom chopping except for the drop shot. My feeling is that chops and slices prolong the rally and that I can finish the point more quickly with my drive and volley. But every stroke can be of use to you at some time or other and it is well to have them all at your call for an emergency or to meet varying conditions of play, particularly until you have mastered the drive to the degree that you can put your full reliance upon speed.

Mix Up Your Speed and Spin

Tilden, with all the great power he brought to bear with both his forehand and backhand drive, still made frequent resort to the chop and the slice. He was possibly the greatest master of spin the game has known, though Norman Brookes of Australia was not far behind, and he could mix up his game with such a variety of strokes that you never knew what to expect next from him. No one was ever better equipped to baffle an opponent or upset him with changes of speed or spin than was Tilden, and no one used his weapons more intelligently or was surer of himself in what he was trying to do. I think that he used spin a little too much when he had so much controlled speed; and if he had gone to the net more often and attached greater emphasis to the volley, he would not have sliced and chopped as much. But the fact is that he did slice and chop and licked the world, and that should be reason enough for anyone wanting to know something about these spin strokes.

Bryan Grant's game illustrates how useful changes of spin and pace can be to a player without great power in his shots. Against an opponent with the blasting speed of Vines, it would be suicide for Bitsy to hit with him. His only chance lies in slowing up the game to give himself more time to get to the ball and in using the kind of shots likely to provoke errors by his opponent. On clay he is particularly effective in the use of a chop and a top-spin drive.

Both the back-spin and the over-spin reduce the speed of the ball, which is not to the liking of a player who thrives on pace. Also, the chop makes for a low bounce and the top-spin for a high one, and the variation may help to unsettle the opponent's stroke.

On the faster surface of grass, Grant uses a flatter stroke or the chop when he wants to attack and the over-spin and chop to defend. His changes of pace and spin, together with his exceptional retrieving ability, sense of anticipation, and rare steadiness have been responsible for his splendid record. His success should be an inspiration to those of short stature who think the little fellow has no chance to get anywhere in tennis. Henri Cochet, William Johnston, Robert Riggs, Gregory Mangin, Berkeley Bell, Wayne Sabin, and Elwood Cooke are no physical giants, either.

Whether or not you make any considerable use of changes of spin or speed, there should always be enough variation to your game to keep the other fellow guessing. Tennis is to be compared to a game of chess in which you seek to outmaneuver the other man and take him off guard or by surprise. If you do the same thing all the time and your opponent does all the thinking, you may lose in spite of a definite superiority in your strokes. The player with great strokes but no "head" is likely to blow up and go to pieces against one who diagnoses his weak points and goes to work on them.

How many times have you seen a young player with wonderful shots, who looks like a world beater in the making, practice against someone who feeds the ball to him? They pop up all the time in every part of the country. But the vast majority of these "phenoms" never get very far. As soon as they get in a tournament match against someone who knows what it is all about and who plays to their weaknesses instead of setting the ball up the way they like it, it becomes apparent that there is nothing behind their shots but steam. There is no plan or purpose. They become rattled and discouraged, and even the merit of their stroke production deserts them as their timing and footwork go off and they are caught out of position.

Every time you go on the court you should have some definite idea of what you intend to do. If you know your man and the strength and weakness of his game, your plan should be all the more clarified. If you are meeting him for the first time and know of his game only by hearsay, it is often wise to devote the first few games to experimenting. Sound him out in an exploratory trip, as it were, to discover the best methods with which to attack.

Although my policy is to attack at all times, it may be that you will decide not to attack, but, instead, to defend. If he is inclined to take chances and allow himself only a small margin of safety, the best thing may be for you to play a waiting game and give him plenty of chances to err.

Your plan should always be flexible and should permit changes as you make new discoveries or find that a particular style of play is not working. In formulating it, you should certainly take into consideration the conditions under which the match is to be played. The type of court, the weather and atmospheric conditions all have a bearing. On grass and dirt, the chop and slice are more effective than on a hard surface, because the spin takes hold and works better. On a wet turf court, they are particularly difficult for the receiver to handle.

I will never forget the lesson Berkeley Bell gave me at Longwood in 1934 in how effective the chop can be in paving the way for a net attack. Without a letup he rushed the net against me behind his chop to defeat me 6-1, 6-0, 6-2. It is true that I had a bad ankle that afternoon, but that did not materially affect the score.

If there is a strong wind blowing, it becomes more difficult for you to control the ball, and spin should be avoided as much as possible, since a crosswind is more likely to catch the ball and deflect its course. The flatly hit shot or the one with a little top-spin will keep a truer direction. If the wind is blowing directly down upon the court, you must hit into it with more force; and with more restraint when it is behind you. Lobs must be carefully calculated lest they hit outside the baseline or fall too short, which is almost as bad against a good smasher. Advantage should be taken of the sun, too, in lobbing. It is particularly difficult for your opponent to make a good overhead when he is looking directly into the sun.

If you are playing on a day of excessive heat, you should nurse your strength carefully and avoid any needless waste of energy. Concentrate all the more on anticipating your opponent's shots to save unnecessary running, and, regardless of the weather, never make a practice of tearing madly after a ball far out of reach unless a particularly vital point is at stake. Even if you should get to the ball and return it, you are likely to be so fagged from your exertions as to lose your control for the next two or three points.

Conserve your energy as much as permissible without jeopardizing your chances of winning. If you are squarely in command of a match and have nothing to fear, it is wise to save yourself as much as possible for the next opponent. Learn to relax. Tension will take almost as much out of you as running. When the point is won or lost, your body should be at ease until the next one begins. This is the practice I follow, and in a tight match it helps to prevent exhaustion from setting in.

The all-court game is the one that brings the most successful results. The player who has all the shots, together with the keen judgment and quick mental reaction under pressure to use them with discrimination, should defeat the player with a limited equipment, other things being equal. There have been players with one or two exceptionally strong shots who have been able to get to the top in spite of deficiencies in other departments, but the records show that tennis has been dominated in recent years by those who have the weapons to attack or stand their ground anywhere on the court, from baseline to net.

Controlled Speed Is Best

Because of the fact that I do not use much variety of spin off the ground, my own game cannot be said to be as completely rounded as was Tilden's, for example. Perhaps had I not concentrated so much on attack, I would have more use for slice and chop; yet, in an all-court attack, I feel I am able to meet the issue wherever it is joined.

The essence of this all-court attack is controlled speed. Your purpose should be to keep the pressure on, but never to strain so much for speed that you sacrifice control. Similarly, never hit a ball any harder than the situation requires; if your opponent is off the court, obviously there is no need for you to kill the ball.

As I mentioned before, an excellent plan of attack is to open up the court through a series of maneuvering plays for the finishing shot at the net. It may not be necessary to go to the net, but in championship-caliber tennis against a foeman worthy of your mettle, remember it is the volley to which you are building up. He, too, will be seeking to get to close quarters; hence, which of you is successful in gaining the volleying position will often be decided by who is able to get in the first telling blow from the back of the court. For this reason, your return of service is of especial importance, though not as much as it is in doubles.

It should be your endeavor with your return of service to nullify the offensive advantage enjoyed by the server. Vincent Richards' object was to do little more than get the ball in play safely with good length, and the regularity with which he handled Tilden's cannonball won him much praise and created a vogue for his method. It is a good policy to follow against the extraordinarily difficult service, with which liberties are taken only at the expense of a large percentage of errors. Most players of the upper flight today are more ambitious with their return.

Fred Perry and Ellsworth Vines often take the wind out of the server's sails, just as Tilden was wont to do himself. It is an intrepid player who rushes to the net behind his service when Perry or Vines is receiving. Their return is so strong that it frequently permits them to wrest the attack from the server forthwith, and I have endeavored to pattern my return after theirs at times, particularly when I want a point badly and my opponent's ground strokes are making it difficult for me to get in.

With the object in mind of getting off on your best foot at the very first stroke, you should contrive to receive the service on your stronger side, usually the forehand with most players. The server, of course, will try to hit to your weakness. By taking your position a little to the left of the center of the court in which you are receiving, you leave a smaller area in which he can direct the ball to your backhand, and you have a better chance to step around the ball and take it on your forehand.

How far back you stand in receiving is determined by the nature of the service and what you propose to do with your return. Ordinarily, you take your position at the baseline or a few inches inside or in back of it. If the serve is unusually fast and flat you may stand a foot or two back, and for a mild second service, a foot or two inside.

If the ball is loaded with the spin of a twist or slice service, breaking wide to the backhand or forehand, respectively, you may be pulled out beyond the sideline to reach it. In that case, you have all the more ground to cover to regain position in the center of the baseline for the next shot. This extra distance might mean the difference between the winning and losing of the rally, and so it is advisable to stand in closer to receive a spin service and take the ball before the "break" has reached its maximum width.

Some players are successful in standing in close and taking a fast, straight service on the rise. Richard Norris Williams went so far on occasion as to meet the ball just behind the service line when he was facing Gerald Patterson of Australia. It was purely a gamble and would get a laugh from the crowd, but Williams figured he had nothing to lose when Patterson's cannonball was scoring aces regularly against him farther back.

A perfect sense of timing and a lightning-quick reflex action are needed to take a cannonball service on the rise. Gene Mako has that action and some of his returns from three feet inside the baseline are breath-taking. Robert Riggs also takes it on the rise at times, but he merely blocks the ball instead of stroking it with Gene's whipping motion. Fred Perry, who takes an early ball as brilliantly as anyone I have ever seen, does it exceptionally well in returning service.

The early return of service is particularly effective when it is brought off well. First of all, it gives the server something to think about and perhaps to worry about when his opponent moves up in the court. He figures that he has to make an even better service than usual; and since the receiver generally goes to the net behind his return because of the unsafe position from which it is made, the server has to worry about that. He either has to resign himself to letting the receiver take the net or, if he determines to go forward himself, he is concerned lest he be caught too far back by a fast, dipping return and have to make a lifting volley.

The psychology of the early return works against the server, but the odds are against the receiver unless he has mastered the timing to Perry's degree and has Fred's wonderful eye and quick reflexes. It is too risky for the average player and my advice is that you be content to receive service farther back at the top of the bound. Once you have acquired consistency in forcing from there, learn to take it on the rise and use the early return of service occasionally for the sake of variation and the psychological effect of worrying your opponent.

The direction of your return of service from the orthodox position depends upon whether or not your opponent follows in to the net, and his strength and weaknesses up there. If he is a net-rusher, there is more pressure on you. Your target is restricted and just a fair shot will not do. Your return must be a winner or strong enough to provoke an error or dislodge your opponent from the attacking position. Above all, you must not give him a high ball to volley. The return must be low, unless it is placed over his head with a lob or down the sideline.

The down-the-line shot is the surest winner if you have the control to penetrate the couple of feet that are beyond the reach of the server laterally. If he should manage to lunge across and volley the ball back, it is difficult for him to recover position in time to get to your next shot. The cross-court return works against players who do not volley angled balls well, but most of them do, returning it straight down. For that reason, I use the angle return sparingly and favor the straight shot, especially from my backhand.

Any fast-dropping, top-spin return of service will do you no harm, and against a server who is slow to get in it is likely to force him to miss in volleying off his ankles or to give you a chance for the down shot. A flat drive of low trajectory is almost as effective. The danger is that you may play these so near the net to avoid giving the server a high volley that you defeat your purpose with an error.

The lob offers a successful alternative at times. It should not be used too often in singles, for its efficacy depends in large part upon the element of surprise. Resort to it when your opponent is least expecting it and is rushing in with nothing on his mind but making a volley.

Hit to His Weakness

Against the server who stays back, the task of the receiver is not so exacting. More time is permitted for him to make his return and the entire court is open to him. He does not have to sight for a narrow opening down the sideline or keep the ball so low, but can play it as safely as he desires, though, of course, nothing is to be gained and much may be lost by merely putting it in play without trying for length, pace, or placement.

The method I employ and advise is to hit deep and with good speed to the server's weak side. Occasionally, if the serve is not too difficult, the ball may be dropped just over the net to trap the server. The deep return to his weakness may elicit from him a short ball that gives you your chance to force him wide of the court for a finishing shot or to gain the net safely for a winning volley.

If his ground strokes are definitely stronger than his service, attack the latter and come in to the net. If he forces equally well with his service and drives, bide your time about going to the net until he gives you a short ball or you have maneuvered him into a defensive position. If he refuses to give you the opportunity to get in and you have not sufficiently mastered the rising ball to use it as an approach shot, change your tactics and endeavor to pull him up with a short, angle shot or a drop shot preparatory to a passing drive or a lob.

In short, keep your thinking cap on and never let your opponent know what to expect next. The variation of your shots and methods and his knowledge that he must be on his toes every instant to cope with your devices are likely to win you his respect and worry him, and that is a part of the psychology of winning tennis.

Psychology, when you come down to it, is a matter of who has confidence and who hasn't. It manifests itself in many ways.

The player who studies the draw sheet before the tournament starts, figures out whom he will probably have to play in each round, and proceeds to get himself in a nervous state about how he is to survive to a certain bracket for the sake of his ranking—that player uses bad psychology and is adding to his troubles. Personally, I steered a course clear of the draw sheet. I never looked to see who was in my half or quarter of the draw. Take them one at a time, and what difference does it make when you meet the tough ones? They have got to be met somewhere along the way; and if you lose to them early, at least you have had profitable experience and competition that should help your game.

Some players work themselves into a state of jitters over the type of court on which the tournament is to be conducted. If they happen to have been brought up on clay or asphalt, and find it difficult at first to adjust themselves to the different reaction of the ball on grass, they become discouraged, decide that turf is not their game, and that they will never be any good on it. That is definitely bad psychology. The battle is half lost before they walk on the court. I made up my mind that I was never going to worry about the surface, that the better player should win on any kind, and that the real champion should be able to adjust his timing and strokes to any speed of the court or balls.

That was the position I took prior to my first professional match with Ellsworth Vines. Many differed with me or thought that I was merely whistling in the dark. They maintained that the strangeness of the indoor conditions at Madison Square Garden would handicap me and that against Ellsworth's great speed I would be unable to find myself until I had gone through the experience of playing at least a few matches under these conditions. I think that the result of the match, which I won 6-3, 6-4, 6-2, supports my contention that you can adapt yourself to any surface, and the player who refuses to believe this simply has no belief in himself.

The player should always be in a composed frame of mind when he is on the court. He has enough to think about in devising ways and means of beating the man across the net to call for the complete concentration of his mental faculties, and anything extraneous or incidental to the actual battle of wits and strokes should be out of his thoughts. Fretting over questionable or even palpably erroneous decisions on the lines or the calling of footfaults against him only works to his greater harm. They create a psychology that is the beginning of a defeatist attitude, which will undermine his confidence and then his control as his resentment affects his concentration and his will to win.

Regardless of whether the decisions are just or unjust, the only sensible thing to do is to take them in stride and forget about them. Once made, they are irrevocable. They are called by men who are trained in their work, and who are doing their duty fairly to the best of their ability. Any experienced player will tell you that any mistakes which are made will even up for the two sides.

To lose your composure over a penalty only doubles or quadruples the significance of the lost point, and there have been occasions when this has changed the course of a match through the victim's refusal to keep his head and heart in the fight. Every beginner should resolve to take the "breaks" as they come, and that includes not only irritating decisions but let-cord balls that tick the tape at the top of the net and fall on the wrong side for him or throw him off his stroke. The player who develops sufficient poise and self-control to take these in stride has made a big step towards the winning psychology. The effect is to be weighed not only upon himself but also upon his opponent, who cannot but be impressed by his refusal to lose heart or concentration. That does not serve to do the opponent's confidence any good, and there is nothing in the rules or unwritten code of tennis that calls for the delivery of any such "service."

9

Doubles

*F*OR SHEER ENJOYMENT, thrills, and satisfaction you can't beat a good game of doubles between two evenly matched teams of the first rank. The sweep and excitement of the play, the animation with which the contestants throw themselves into their work, the jockeying and fencing for openings, and the reverberation of the overhead smash all combine to keep the spectators on the edges of their seats.

There is more fun in doubles, both for the players and the spectators. The situations lend themselves to the comedy of the too-ambitious effort that back-fires; there is the bafflement and pained confusion of the side that is outfoxed and runs in the wrong direction or into the cannon's mouth. At least the opponents can see the humor of the situation which brings a ripple of chuckles or an explosive roar of mirth from the stands.

There is no satisfaction, of course, like winning a championship solely on your own individual efforts in singles, but in doubles I think you are inclined to feel a little more pleased with yourself. You experience a deep glow of pleasure that is reflected in the happy smiles usually wreathing the faces of the winning pair as they advance to shake hands with their opponents at the end.

There is a reason for this. Doubles is so much a test of

craft and finesse, and the penalty for a poor shot is so heavy that you have to be on your toes mentally every moment the ball is in play. The relaxing of this mental strain and your gratification over beating the other side as much with your head as with your hand results in a very pleasurable reaction.

The comradeship that develops on the doubles court also enters into the explanation. You rejoice in the success of your partner as well as your own. Usually, there is a very close bond of friendship between the members of a team if the two have played together for any considerable period. Wilmer Allison and John Van Ryn became almost inseparable after forming their alliance in 1928, and so deep are the roots of their mutual regard that John moved from Philadelphia to Texas to go into business with Wilmer.

I cite the instance of Allison and Van Ryn to emphasize how important it is that the members of a doubles team get along well together both on and off the court. They stand as one of the great combinations of tennis, and their loyalty to each other and their complete accord were unquestionable factors in their success.

Doubles is a game in which two players must dovetail their efforts into a smoothly functioning unit which will present an invulnerable front and which will coördinate operations of the attack. Each must be ready and willing to submerge his individuality for the good of the team in a spirit of one for all and all for one. To achieve complete harmony of action, there must be no discordant note of personal feeling. The stronger the tie of friendship between two players, the more readily each sacrifices the natural craving for individual glory in order to contribute to teamwork and the collective good. Each endeavors to set up the winning shot for the other, rather than assert himself at the expense of sound position play.

Because of the necessity for this harmony on the court, I strongly advise that in choosing a partner for doubles you select someone with whom you can get along—a friend or someone with whom you have something in common. Even if he is not as good a player as another that you might join forces with, it will repay you in the long run, and you will get more thrill and fun out of winning.

Stick to one partner unless you find after a fair trial that you are not getting results and you become convinced that your games will not blend because of common weaknesses. The older the partnership the smoother will be your teamwork, which should eventually become instinctive, and the more confidence you will have in each other and in yourselves as a unit.

Almost without exception, the great teams have been those that have remained fixtures year after year. Some of these are Holcombe Ward and Dwight F. Davis, Ward and Beals C. Wright, Fred B. Alexander and Harold Hackett, Maurice McLoughlin and Thomas Bundy, William Johnston and Clarence Griffin, Howard and Robert Kinsey, William Tilden and Vincent Richards, Richards and Richard Norris Williams, and Allison and Van Ryn. Gene Mako and I kept our partnership unbroken from the time we first joined forces, and Berkeley Bell and Gregory Mangin, though they never won the championship, were an exceedingly difficult team to beat because they played together so constantly as well as because of their fiery aggressiveness.

George Lott furnished an exception in that he swapped

partners four times and won at least one championship with each of them. With John Hennessey, John Doeg, and Lester Stoefen he won the national title five times, and with Van Ryn, in their first season together, the French and British crowns. Lott was such a great doubles player in his stroke equipment and his tactical skill that he would have been a hard man to beat no matter who was playing alongside him. He was not fickle to his partners, but played with them as long as each of them was available.

Hennessey, from whom he acquired his rare knack of disguising his lob to look like his drive, had to give up the game because of trouble with his feet. Doeg withdrew from tournament competition after they had failed in their effort to win the national championship a third successive time. Lott joined forces with Van Ryn on an overseas campaign in 1931 at the request of the Davis Cup Committee—a temporary arrangement in the absence of Allison—and later came his partnership with Stoefen, with whom he won the national crown twice before they entered the professional ranks.

Lott Excelled in Doubles

The doubles game is a different proposition from singles and Lott's success with four different partners is to be explained by the fact that his shots and methods were so perfect that he was able to adapt them to anything his partner had to offer. Hennessey, with his looping, Western drive, his mildly hit service, his generally soft game and his sagacity; Doeg, with his terrific service and effectiveness at the net in murdering the setups extracted by

Lott's tactics; Stoefen, with the same strong points and a hard, flat return of service that Doeg lacked; and Van Ryn, with his sound all-round game, featured by the regularity of his return of service, the industry and accuracy with which he backed up his partner, and his quickness in making volley interceptions of the lifting returns provoked by Lott's artful "dink" shot—all of them, with their different styles, became champions with Lott, though only one of them won the singles title.

Lott, himself, never was able to win the championship alone, though he was runner-up to Vines in 1931, but he is generally ranked as the greatest doubles player of his time. Players who have had less success in singles than Lott have made their mark in doubles, while some who have been singles champions were never outstanding on the larger court. Van Ryn, Griffin, Hackett, the Kinsey brothers, and Hennessey are examples in the first category, as are Gledhill, Stoefen, Bundy, and Alexander. On the other hand, Fred Perry and Mrs. Helen Wills Moody, two of the greatest singles champions of modern times, have not excelled in anything like the same degree at the four-handed game.

All this should make it clear that doubles and singles are different games, even though there are any number of players who have played brilliant tennis in both. Some of these are Mrs. George W. Wightman, Miss Mary K. Browne, Mrs. Sarah Palfrey Fabyan, and Miss Alice Marble, and Tilden, Williams, Johnston, McLoughlin, Richards, Allison, and Vines. Some of the tennis experts contend that Tilden was not a first-class doubles player, but his record in winning the championship five times with

Richards, B. I. C. Norton, and Francis Hunter argues differently.

The reason for the failure of some highly successful singles players to excel in doubles has been the absence of variation from their game, their lack of the strokes that pay the biggest dividends, or their inability to coördinate their efforts with someone else. The sheer speed of straight hitting is not enough, no matter how accurate, fast of foot, or perfectly trained you may be.

Doubles is a game of finesse and scheming, of constant fencing for openings, of baiting and trapping your opponents, of maneuvering them into faulty position to expose a vulnerable point, or to extract a setup for the finishing thrust. Speed plays its part, but subtlety, shading, discernment in detecting the weak spot in the opposing formation, and quickness to choose and carry out the correct procedure in attacking it are even more important. Also, one must have plenty of patience in working up to the finishing thrust.

With two players defending the court, openings are not so easy to find as in singles, and where you place the ball is of more consequence. In singles, a good proportion of the points are won from the back of the court with straight hitting. In doubles, it is at the net that almost all of the scoring is done. The efforts and strategy of each team are directed toward gaining and holding command of the net. The team that is up to the net endeavors to remain entrenched until it has forced the opponents to return the ball above the level of the net where it can be volleyed or smashed decisively. The team that is back seeks to dislodge the other with deep lobs that drive them back or with low, dipping returns to their feet that compel them to volley up, thus permitting the back pair to challenge their position or put them to rout by rushing in and volleying down. The down shot is the big winner because at least one team is always at the net from the time the server follows in behind his delivery until the rally is ended. So every ball hit from the back of the court must be kept low unless it is a lob.

The service, the return of service, the volley, the half volley, the lob, and the smash all get a lot of play in doubles. Which is the most important is a matter of personal opinion and difficult to say.

There can be no question, it seems to me, that the service and the return of service are fully as important as any of the others, if not more so. The service must give safe approach to the net; and, if it does not permit the server to get in close enough, he may be beaten by a return to his feet. If the service is weak, the return may force the server to make a lifting volley or a half volley that will give the opponents a chance to hit down from the very start of the rally, and possibly win the point at once.

Reversing the situation, the return of service must be a good shot or the server, rushing to the net, will be given the opportunity for a put-away volley, or his partner, stationed at the net, may step across to volley the ball out of reach. Thus, both the service and the return of service have a significant bearing on which side gets in the first telling blow. The advantage, of course, lies with the serving side, but the return of service can nullify it and give the other pair command at the net.

The importance of the volley is obvious from the fact that both teams strive to get to the net, where the great majority of the points are won. The server not only has to be able to lift a fast-dropping ball while coming in, but he also has to be skilled in the half volley. The lob, one of the chief devices for driving back a volleying pair and often for splitting their formation, is frequently used to return the serve. The fact that it is resorted to frequently establishes, *ipso facto,* the importance of the smash in answering it and retaining the attacking position in the forecourt.

The advantage enjoyed by the serving side in its primary command of the net is so marked that "breaks" through service are few and far between as a rule when two first-class pairs are matched. The loss of its service is a definite psychological handicap to a team for this reason. The odds are against evening up the score, and one such loss generally decides the outcome of the set. As a result, it is customary for a team to concentrate on winning its services, and to relax a bit when receiving until opportunity calls in the way of a lucky stroke or a slip-up by the opponents.

Make the First Ball Good

Assuming that you and your partner are serving, that you are "on offense," remember a cardinal rule of doubles: the server should get his first ball in play. Lott was a stickler for this. He not only practiced it, but he preached it to his partner. He insisted on it so much that he advocated the use of the second service as the first if his partner got only a small percentage of his fast first serves in play. His reason, and a good one, is that the receiver usually stands a foot to three feet farther back for the first serve than he does for the second, and the farther back he is, the more time the server has to get to the net.

So, instead of trying for a cannonball, it is better in doubles to use a medium-paced, well-placed first service with spin on the ball. Occasionally, you can mix in a fast one to keep the receiver guessing and to discourage him from inching up, but make it a point to get the first ball inside the line. The medium-speed ball gives you more time to get to the net, and the spin helps you control the ball and place it on your opponent's weak side.

I find an American twist service does the job well. The "kick" is to the receiver's backhand, which is usually his weaker side, and the break pulls him wide, particularly in the left court. This service delays his return, thus giving you more time to gain the volleying position. If he moves to his left to receive, in order to step around the ball and hit it on the forehand, play a slice or a fast flat serve to his right once in a while. That will make him more careful about covering up his backhand too much.

Your object on your service is to prevent the receiver from forcing you into making a difficult low volley and to extract from him a ball above the level of the net that you can hit down. The position of your partner is important in helping you to protect the service by restricting the range of the return. He should be stationed close to the net and as far to the inside as possible without leaving more than a foot or two of the alley uncovered. In this position, he forces the receiver to return the service cross-court to you or to throw up a lob. Any other return would be within the reach of your partner's volley unless the receiver gambled on a passing shot straight down the alley.

Nine times out of ten the ball comes back to the server

unless it is a lob. If he is slow in running up, and the return is a low flat drive or a fast-dropping top-spin shot, he must lift it with his volley or half volley. If he meets the ball quickly well inside the service line, he has a better chance to make a forcing volley. But regardless of where he meets the return, he should continue on his way forward after his volley to seek better position for the second one, always alert for a lob from the opponents.

In making this first volley, he will find that the center theory works nicely. His shot down the middle of the court will draw either one or both opponents there and thus expose one or both corners of the court to his second volley, at the same time closing off his own court to an angled drive.

This first volley should be played safely unless, of course, you have a high ball to deal with. It should be hit low, with back-spin, to prevent the opponents from hitting down. Your purpose is not to win with the first volley, as in singles, but to entrench yourself in the forecourt, and pave the way for a down shot on the second or third volley.

If the return of service is a lob, either you or your partner falls back for it. Quite often it will be tossed over your partner's head. It is good practice for each man to cover lobs to his own side, but some teams reach an agreement for one or the other to cover all that he can take comfortably. Once you smash down the lob, return immediately to join your partner at the net.

If the lob is a deep one, so carefully concealed that it takes you both by surprise, and can just barely be retrieved on the bounce with a defensive return, you and your partner should both fall back. Your opponents, if

they are playing heads-up doubles, have come up with
their lob and are at the net ready to volley, or to smash if
your return is also a lob. You and your partner have a
better chance to resist their volley or smash at the baseline
than you would have with either of you braving their fire
at close quarters. They have now taken over the attack
and have forced you on the defensive; you, in turn, seek to
dislodge them with lobs or low top-spin drives.

Regarding the defense, there is first the formation for
receiving service. The partner of the receiver can take
one of several positions. He can stand at a spot just inside the service court if the server usually hits the first
ball mildly. This is known as the Australian formation of
one up and one back. When the receiver has made a low
cross-court drive wide of the server's partner at the net, its
merit lies in the fact that it compels the server to make a
strong, low, cross-court volley. If he volleys up, the receiver, who is coming in fast, or his partner at the net will
intercept the ball for a point-winning volley.

If the serve is known to be fast, the receiver's partner stands just inside the baseline, prepared for a deep
volley of the return by the server. If the first service is a
fault, the partner then moves up to the service court for
the second ball. This is the procedure that Mako and I
followed.

Many of the foreign teams at one time used the Australian formation almost exclusively, concentrating on forcing the server to volley up by taking the service on the
rise, and shooting fast for his feet. Against Americans
this formation did not work out so well because of the difficulty they had in handling the serves of such players
as Tilden, Williams, Allison, Doeg, Lott, Stoefen, and

Vines, and keeping the return low. Recently, however, there has been a more general international style as a result of the exchange of ideas and the experience gained in Davis Cup play.

Shoot for Their Feet

The receivers, as I stated before, are at a disadvantage because they do not get their first crack at the ball until their opponents are already in volleying position. Their return is thereby restricted, and there is practically no chance to score with the first stroke as in singles unless daring chances are taken straight down the alley, or unless an exceptionally brilliant low drive down the middle or short and wide across court into the alley is brought off. The open space is so limited that it calls for a big gamble to effect a winner.

The next best thing is (1) returning the ball across court with top-spin to the feet of the server in order to extract an error or a lifting volley that gives the receivers the opportunity to run in and volley down, or (2) throwing up a lob. The purpose is to wrest the net position away from the serving side, and to inveigle them into setting up a ball for a down-shot.

A medium-paced shot to the feet is an excellent return, for it not only compels the server to volley up, but it prevents him from getting much pace on his ball. Lott was a master at this, and his slow "dink" shot, which Mako also uses extremely well, set up more winners than almost any other in his repertory, although his lob was a thorn in the side of his opponents, too.

George played the dink softly, disguising it so well that

you could not tell whether he was going to drive, lob, or dink. Off a fast service, of course, the dink was not practicable and he brought his fast, top-spin forehand into play with one of the best returns of service from the left court I have seen, or he hit his backhand at an effective angle or threw up a marvelously concealed lob. But against a moderate second service and a slow-footed net-rusher the dink would get his opponents into hot water time and again.

Lott used it not only in returning service but any time in the rally when the opponents showed the tendency to play back a little too far from the net. With the same motion that he used for the drive and the lob, he played the ball gently with a delicate touch, and at an angle to drop at the feet of the opponent.

With Doeg or Stoefen or Van Ryn stationed at the net and ready to cut off the return, the receiver of the dink usually had to play the ball off balance to Lott or to throw up a lob as best he could, giving George the opportunity for a finishing volley or smash or at least to join his partner at the net. After the opponents had had a few samples of the dink, they would decide to play closer to the net for their volleys and thus avoid being trapped by the ball at their feet, unless they had the anticipation and speed of Wilmer Allison, who could tear for the net to volley the dink before it started to drop. Once they camped on top of the net they found that it was a case of out of the frying pan into the fire, for Lott's lob was just as troublesome as his dink.

As I stated earlier, the lob is much more effective in doubles than it is in singles. The Kinsey brothers won the national championship through their ability to stand be-

Note the tension as Budge makes a low backhand volley in the 1937 Davis
Cup challenge round doubles. Budge and Mako defeated Charles Tuckey and
Frank Wilde of Great Britain.

Budge is about to make an overhead smash as he joins Mako in the forecourt
after serving. This action took place in the Davis Cup interzone round against
Von Cramm and Henkel of Germany, July 19, 1937.

hind the baseline and toss the ball into the air until their more aggressive opponents became arm weary from smashing and erred or gave them the chance to come in on one of Howard's famous loop-drives.

But the lob is more than a defensive measure in the four-handed game. It is one of your best bets for gaining the commanding position. It is a real comfort against a strong volleying team with big serves and, as executed by Lott and Bobby Riggs, it can be almost demoralizing.

Lott and Riggs both use the lob so well in singles that it becomes an offensive weapon. In doubles Lott, because he masks the shot so cleverly, takes the opponents by surprise, keeps the ball just out of reach, and puts top-spin on it to get a nice pitch, often has thrown the other side into confusion. Keith Gledhill, Bitsy Grant, Wayne Sabin, and Gilbert Hall have also been unusually good lobbers, and Mako, with his wonderfully quick reflex action, has trapped the opposition cold at the net with his lob volley, one of the riskiest of shots.

In our defense against the lob, Gene and I always tried to kill any ball between the net and the service line. Anything farther back than that, we played more carefully, waiting for a better opportunity, although Gene specializes in killing a lob rising from the ground in deep court.

Gene is pretty much of the specialist all-round. His service is hit mildly and his return of service is not always accurate, but he has so many surprises up his sleeve, he acts with such lightning quickness at the net, and has so much confidence in doing the unexpected and daring that the opponents are on tenterhooks as to what he is going to pull off next. His drop volleys, dink shots, use of angles, variations, smashing and lobbing, combined with my power and straighter hitting, made for success because of the changes of pace and wide range of shots.

Gene is an individualist, but he plays for the team and not the limelight, and I could always depend upon him to cover me up any time I left my position. He seemed to anticipate my moves, and whatever success came our way was owing in no small part to the smoothness with which we fitted our games together and complemented each other. Each of us could sense almost instinctively what was in the other's mind and so we moved as a unit in carrying out attacking operations or falling into a defensive formation. This coördination can come only from an enduring association, and so let me urge again the advisability of selecting the right partner and clinging to him.

Partners in doubles should not only complement but also compliment each other. Carping and quibbling can ruin your teamwork. Refrain from criticizing each other's mistakes and sulking. The resentment that is thereby created ruins the confidence of both you and your partner, and mars your concentration. Even when things are not going well, be pleasant to one another and encourage rather than find fault.

When the baseball pitcher is having a bad inning, his teammates come in and reaffirm their faith in him to steady his nerves and bolster his confidence. The same spirit of loyalty should be shown on the tennis court. You will win more matches, and you will have a lot more fun.

When the game ceases to be fun, a player should cut the gut out of his racquets and put them in storage. He is taking it much too seriously.

10

Getting Personal

LAWN TENNIS HAS always been an exemplar of the highest type of sportsmanship. The spirit of fair play permeates the game and is one of its most cherished traditions. No one can long be associated with tennis and not be conscious of it. It is not confined to the players and the court. It manifests itself on every side in the bearing and acts of all connected with the sport.

The executives who direct the destinies of the game, the tournament officials who conduct the various competitions, and the umpires and linesmen who sit in judgment upon the strokes of the matches all play their parts in this spirit and take pride in the heritage. The spectators who watch from the stands observe the spirit in their demonstrations and particularly in the consideration they show for players from abroad in Davis Cup and Wightman Cup matches. The press and radio are guided by it in their accounts of the play.

The young player starting out in tennis should bend his earliest steps towards strict conformance not only to the rules but to the unwritten code of fair play. There is little place in tennis for anyone who does not. He soon finds himself so out of favor with his fellow players, the officials, the gallery, and the press that his career likely will be a short one and an unhappy one.

153

It has been my observation that the great majority of tennis players require no lessons in good sportsmanship. Their background, instincts, home influence, and school discipline have eliminated any need for corrective measures. This is true not only of tennis but of most games with which I am familiar. Fair play is the cardinal rule.

But occasionally a player comes along who is the exception. Either through faulty temperament, or lack of understanding, or an urge to win that blinds him to the error of his ways, he deliberately or unknowingly violates the code and gets everyone down on him. His transgressions may be within the letter of the law, but it is the infringement upon the spirit of the rules that is most to be condemned.

First of all, the beginner should procure a copy of the rules of lawn tennis and thoroughly familiarize himself with them. This will serve for his own protection and interests as well as to assist him to keep clearly in mind the rights of his opponent. There is a copy of the rules in the appendix of this volume.

A careful inspection of the footfault rule is particularly recommended. There is no other in the code which is more frequently violated, usually unintentionally. Footfaults are not always called. In the case of a player who habitually makes them, to penalize every one of them would ruin the match. Some players, aware of this tendency towards leniency, take advantage of it at the expense of their opponents. That is hardly in keeping with the spirit of fair play.

Another unfortunate practice is stalling. Some players are guilty of this without thinking about it. Others are not so innocent. It manifests itself in their taking unduly long to take their position between points, and in excessive delay at the umpire's stand in changing courts while they dry their hands and face, quench their thirst, or pour water over their heads on a hot day.

Some will drop into a chair and remain there until cautioned by the umpire. Perhaps they will slowly unlace and lace up their shoes, carefully comb their hair, engage the umpire in conversation, or go through their stock of racquets, testing each one for its stringing, to make a new selection. Some take their time about recovering balls on the court or off at a distance; and if ball boys are provided, the latter are told by the server not to bounce the balls to him but to wait until he walks up to the boys to take them.

Avoid Unfair Delays

A few players resort to anything to hold up the play so they can catch their breath or take the strain off their weary limbs for one or two extra moments. As tennis is a test not only of playing ability but also of physical condition, such tactics are manifestly unfair to the opponent, whose plan of strategy may be centered in tiring the other man.

Holding up the opponent's second service by taking unduly long to get back into position after stepping to the side for a faulty first ball is also unfair. There is a certain rhythm and timing between the first and second ball, and this is lost to the server by such tactics. Knocking the first ball back at the server when it is a fault is also to be shunned when possible for the same reason. On the other hand, the server should not hurry his second ball when the opponent has been pulled away by a faulty first serve, but should give the latter time to return to his position and get set. Common, ordinary courtesy dictates this.

Challenging the decisions of the linesmen and footfault judge or even the mere facial expression of disgust over them is a bad habit and in poor taste. The officials do their job to the best of their ability, and they do it without pay and without favoritism. They are only human and may make mistakes the same as anyone else; but it should be remembered that they are in the best possible position to see exactly where the ball strikes, they are trained and experienced, and what mistakes they do make, if any, are likely to be equalized for each side.

Unless the official's calls are so flagrantly wrong that there can be no possible doubt of his incompetency and his decisions are ruining the match for the players and spectators, any slightest expression of reproof should be avoided. It is a reflection upon the linesman and creates resentment which disturb his concentration. It is also bad for the player; anyone who protests decisions and nurses a grudge against an official is not helping his own concentration. The smart thing to do is to take them as they are called and put them out of mind.

The throwing of points to make up for decisions against the opponent that appear to be erroneous is to be approved in one respect but challenged in another. It is evidence of the thrower's spirit of fairness and invariably it meets with a warm demonstration of approval from the gallery. At the same time it is a slap at the linesman, who may have been right; and if there is any question in the opponent's mind as to whether it was necessary, he may, in turn, throw a point. The gallery applauds and chuckles, and by the time the players get down to serious business again one or both may find his concentration has wavered.

It is all very nice and friendly, but hard on the official, and it is good policy for players to decide before a match not to throw points but to take the calls as they come. Where there is no question in a player's mind or anyone else's that an injustice has been done, let him throw the point if he must, but let him do it as unostentatiously as possible. He may feel uncomfortable if he does not throw it, but he should think how badly the official feels if he does.

It is the natural desire of everyone who appears in public to make the best possible impression. The tennis player, in this connection, is judged not only by his bearing and conduct but also by his neatness. The player who is careless and slovenly in his dress and appears on the court in shorts or flannels that are stained with dirt or from contact with the turf and are long overdue at the cleaner's, or wears a soiled shirt or dirty shoes, does himself an injustice. He can hardly help being conscious of the unsightly figure he makes by contrast with his immaculately attired opponent, and if he is at all sensitive it may affect his concentration to some degree.

One need not be a Beau Brummell on the court and there is no occasion for him to visit Fifth Avenue for the latest mode in tennis wardrobes. All that he requires are enough changes of clothes to assure that the laundry will turn him out properly for each appearance on the court. A half dozen shirts, preferably of the pull-over type, three or four pairs of flannels or shorts, two pairs of sneakers or lightweight shoes with flat, rubber soles (or one pair and a tube of white cleaner), a half dozen pairs of woolen socks and a pull-over sweater should be in the equipment of the tournament player. White is the prescribed color for tennis. Dress for comfort and particularly avoid wearing tight-fitting shoes.

In selecting a racquet avoid picking one that is too heavy, for the extra weight may be a burden in a long match. At the same time don't go to the other extreme, for the weight of the head does a part of the work in giving momentum to the shot. I personally like a heavy racquet of 15 ounces, but the average weight is about 13 or 13½. Pick a racquet that feels a bit heavier than just right, for it won't feel that same way when you swing it at a ball.

A Good Racquet Is a 'Must'

The beginner need not buy the most expensive racquet; but if he takes good care of it, the best will cost no more in the end than a cheaper one. The better frame will have better balance, and a good quality of gut is especially desirable. It will last two to three times as long as cheap gut. The type of gut to be used depends upon the surface of the court. On a gritty court, where sand is picked up by the strings, it should be coarser than the gut used on other surfaces. The tightness of the stringing is determined by the type of game you play. The tighter the stringing, the harder the face and the faster the shot, and also the more difficult it is to control the ball.

For the beginner, a moderately tight stringing is recommended, as well as for those who use a great deal of spin on the ball. The looser the stringing, the longer the ball stays on the face of the racquet.

Regardless of how expensive a racquet you buy, it will not serve you long unless you treat it right. Be careful about using it in wet weather, since rain is bad for the gut. Dry it off with a towel or cloth when any moisture has gathered on it and, when it is not in use, keep it in a weather-proof covering and a screw-press. Otherwise you may pick it up some day and find that some of the strings have snapped or the frame has warped. In other words, give it the thought and care that a hunter gives to his gun.

Physical condition is a big factor in winning tennis. The player who hopes to make any headway in tournament competition must keep himself in first-class shape and give thought to his food and rest. No stringent regulations need be followed and no great sacrifices are called for; but there are some things that have to be given up, and regular habits must be cultivated.

Plenty of sleep, particularly before an important match, is almost indispensable. After a good night's sleep, the rested feeling adds to your confidence. Spacing your meals and eating at regular intervals are also beneficial. I make it a practice to eat two hours before I go on the court.

Eating the correct things, too, is important, as I found out through my weakness for a tempting tid-bit purveyed at all sporting events. Anything fried should be off the menu, and lobster, shrimp, pork and cucumbers do not sit well on the stomach when tearing after a lob or a drop shot. Eating anything in sight at any time does not do you any good in tournament tennis, any more than it does in running the hundred-yard dash. You do a lot more running in the course of a match than any track man does. If you aren't able to deny yourself a piece of pastry, how can you fail to get upset over bad decisions? It is all a matter of will power and self-control.

The tennis player who gets sufficient sleep, uses common sense in eating, and, of course, abstains from spirits, need have no worries about his physical condition. There are certain exercises, however, that may prove beneficial. I find that to lie on the floor flat on my back and lift my legs 25 times is good for the stomach muscles. But don't do it if you have been inactive for a long period.

On our trip to Australia in late 1937, Gene Mako and I decided to do our exercises. We hadn't touched a racquet or used our legs for anything more strenuous than dancing for six weeks; consequently we got so stiff that we couldn't move on the court.

We simply didn't use any judgment, and judgment is something the tennis player must have if he wants to win. One doesn't have to be a mental heavyweight to be a champion. All he needs is to exercise average intelligence. The dub of today who does that may be the champion of tomorrow, if he is willing to work and not just play tennis. If anything I have set down previously in these pages may have led you to believe differently—that one must be a phenomenon to be a champion—a "grand slam" is in order, and my apologies. I won't say another word.

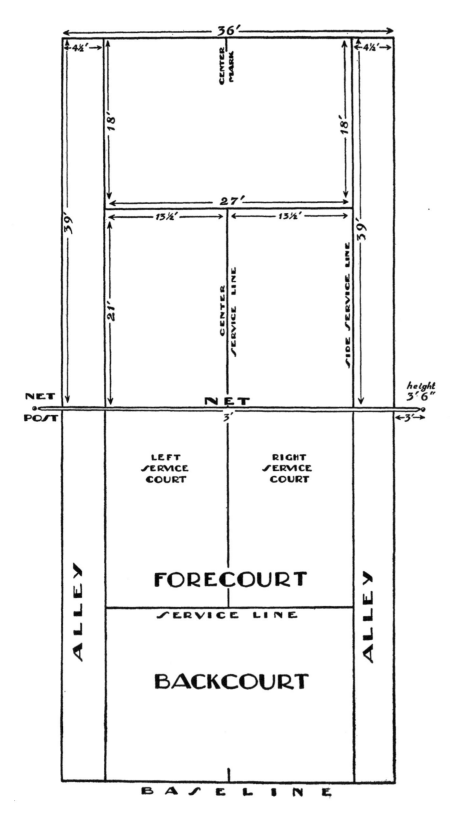

LAWN TENNIS COURT

This diagram illustrates the court for the doubles game; the regulations for a singles court are explained in Rule 1, pages 164-165. *See also* the *Explanation of Rule 1*, page 165.

The court should lie north and south in order to give the best protection from the direct rays of the sun.

Appendix

The glossary of technical terms and the rules of lawn tennis and cases and decisions are printed with the consent and through the courtesy of the United States Lawn Tennis Association.

Glossary of Technical Terms

NET—The netting placed across the middle of the court.

POST—One of the wooden or metal uprights supporting the net.

BAND—The strip of canvas attached to the top of the net.

BASE LINE—The back line at either end of the court.

SIDE LINE—The line at either side of the court that marks the outside edge of the playing surface.

SERVICE LINE—The line 21 feet from the net that bounds the back of the service courts.

CENTER SERVICE LINE—The line dividing the service court into halves and separating the right and left service courts.

CENTER MARK—The mark bisecting the base line, defining one of the limits of the service position.

SIDE SERVICE LINE—The line forming the boundary of the service courts at the right and left sides. In singles the side service lines are also part of the side lines.

TO SERVE—To put the ball into play.

SERVICE, OR SERVE—The act of putting the ball into play.

SERVER—The player who serves.

RECEIVER—The player who receives the service.

TOSS—To spin or throw up the racket for choice of service or court.

FAULT—A served ball that does not strike in the proper court, or is not properly served.

FOOT FAULT—Position or movements of the feet before or during the service in violation of Rule 6.

VOLLEY—A stroke made by hitting a ball before it has touched the ground, except in serving.

RACKET—The implement used to strike the ball.

LET—A served ball that touches the net and yet goes into the proper court. Also any stroke that does not count and is played over.

STROKE—The act of striking the ball with the racket.

PERMANENT FIXTURES—The umpire, linesmen and spectators, and their chairs or stands, net, posts, back and side-stops, and any other objects situated around a court. (Also see note to Playing Rule No. 20.)

IN PLAY—A ball is "in play" from the instant it leaves the server's hands until the point has been decided.

POINT—The smallest unit of the score. Four points scored win a game, unless both sides have won three points, when the score is "deuce" and one side must gain a lead of two points to win the game.

GAME—The unit of scoring next higher than the point, scored when either side has won four points, unless the other side has meantime won three; in that case the side first gaining a lead of two points wins.

SET—The unit of scoring next higher than the game, scored when either side has won six games, unless the other side has meantime won five; in that case the side first gaining a lead of two games wins.

UMPIRE—The official in charge of the match, whose duties are defined in the regulations.

REFEREE—The official in charge of a tournament, whose duties are defined in the U.S.L.T.A. tournament regulations.

LINESMAN—An official of the match, whose duties are defined in the U.S.L.T.A. tournament regulations.

TOURNAMENT—An official competition.

TOURNAMENT COMMITTEE—The committee in charge of a tournament.

CHALLENGE CUP—A trophy placed in competition under stated conditions, which must be won more than once.

Rules of Lawn Tennis
and
Cases and Decisions

EXPLANATORY NOTE

The appended Code of Rules is the Official Code of the International Lawn Tennis Federation, of which the United States Lawn Tennis Association is a member.

The Cases and Decisions, the Glossary of Terms and the Tournament Regulations are addenda adopted by the United States Lawn Tennis Association and are official in the United States only, although they in no way conflict with the Code or international practice.

The Explanations while *not official* utterances may be considered a correct guide for interpreting the Rules. They have been prepared by the Tennis Umpires Association to amplify and explain the formal Code.

THE SINGLES GAME

RULE 1.—The *Court* shall be a rectangle 78 feet long and 27 feet wide. It shall be divided across the middle by a net, suspended from a cord or metal cable of a maximum diameter of one-third of an inch, the ends of which shall be attached to, or pass over, the tops of two posts, 3 feet 6 inches high, which shall stand 3 feet outside the court on each side. The height of the net shall be 3 feet at the center, where it shall be held down taut by a strap not more than 2 inches wide. There shall be a band covering the cord or metal cable and the top of the net for not less than 2 inches nor more than 2½ inches in depth on each side. The lines bounding the ends and sides of the court shall respectively be called the *Base Lines* and the *Side Lines*. On each side of the net, at a distance of 21 feet from it and parallel with it, shall be drawn the *Service Lines*. The space on each side of the net between the service line and the side lines shall be divided into two equal parts called the *Service Courts* by the *Center Service Line*, which must be 2 inches in width, drawn half-way between, and parallel with, the side lines. Each base line shall be bisected by an imaginary continuation of the center service line to a line 4 inches in length and 2 inches in width called the *Center Mark*, drawn inside the court and at right angles to and in contact with such base line. All other lines shall be not less than 1 inch nor more than 2 inches in width, except the base lines, which may be 4 inches in width, and all measurements shall be made to the outside of the lines.

Note—In the case of the International Lawn Tennis Championship (Davis Cup) or other official championships of the International Federation, there shall be a space behind each base line of not less than 21 feet, and at the sides of not less than 12 feet.

Explanation of Rule 1

The posts in singles should be 3 feet outside the singles court, and in doubles 3 feet outside the doubles court.

The net should be 33 feet wide for a singles court, and 42 feet wide for a doubles court. It should touch the ground along its entire length and come flush to the posts at all points.

It is well to have a stick 3 feet 6 inches long, with a notch cut in at the 3-foot mark, for the purpose of measuring the height of the net at the posts and in the center. These measurements, as well as the measurements of the court itself, always should be made before starting to play an important match.

RULE 2.—The permanent fixtures of the court shall include not only the nets, posts, cord or metal cable, strap and band, but also, where there are any such, the back and side stops, the stands, fixed or movable seats and chairs round the court, and their occupants, all other fixtures around and above the court, and the Umpire, Foot Fault Judge and Linesmen when in their respective places.

RULE 3.—The ball shall have a smooth outer surface, seams in the cover shall be stitchless. The ball shall be more than two and a-half inches and less than two and five-eighths inches in diameter, and more than two ounces and less than two and one-sixteenth ounces in weight. The ball shall have a bound of more than 53 inches and less than 58 inches when dropped 100 inches upon a concrete base, and a deformation of more than .265 of an inch and less than .290 of an inch when subjected to a pressure of 18 lbs. applied to each end of any diameter. All tests shall be made in accordance with the official regulations.

CASE I. Should a ball become broken through hitting, shall a let be called?

Decision. Yes.

Explanation of Rule 3

"How often may the players have new balls?" is a question that is frequently asked.

According to Tournament Regulation 14 (g) the Umpire, subject to the approval of the Referee, may decide when new balls are required to insure fairness of playing conditions. In matches where there is no Umpire, the players should agree beforehand on this matter.

RULE 4.—The players shall stand on opposite sides of the net; the player who first delivers the ball shall be called the *Server*, and the other the *Receiver*.

CASE II. A player returns the ball, and finding that he cannot stop himself before reaching the net, jumps over it. Is it a good return?

Decision. No. Rule 4 requires that the players shall be on opposite sides of the net, and therefore the player invading his opponent's court loses the stroke.

CASE III. The Server claims that the Receiver must stand in the court. Is this necessary?

Decision. No. The Receiver may stand wherever he pleases on his own side of the net.

CASE IV. A cuts the ball just over the net and it returns to A's side. B, unable to reach the ball, throws his racket and hits the ball. Both racket and ball fall over the net on A's court. A returns the ball outside of B's court. Who wins the point?

Decision. When B threw his racket across the net he invaded his opponent's territory and such an invasion was in a measure responsible for A's returning the ball out of court; in other words, B would lose the point.

CASE V. A player in returning the ball, which has been played just over the net with a heavy cut so that it bounces sharply to one side and backward, runs outside the court, and, while the ball is still in play, passes the imaginary line which would be made by the extension of the net. Technically, he is not on his side of the net, and Rule 4 states that players shall be on opposite sides of the net. Does he lose the point:

(*a*) If he strikes the ball before stepping across the imaginary line which would be made by the extension of the net?

(*b*) If he strikes the ball after stepping across the imaginary line?

Decision. He does not lose the point in either case, unless he actually gets in his opponent's way and hinders his return.

RULE 5.—The choice of sides and the right to be Server or Receiver in the first game shall be decided by toss.

The player winning the toss may choose, or request his opponent to choose:

(a) the right to be Server or Receiver, in which case the other player shall choose the side; or

(b) the side in which case the other player shall choose the right to be Server or Receiver.

Explanation of Rule 5

The toss is usually made by one player twirling a racket in the air, the other calling "Rough" or "Smooth"; which means that the fine stringing (the trimming) at the head of the racket will have the rough or the smooth side up when the racket falls to the ground.

RULE 6.—The service shall be delivered in the following manner. Immediately before commencing to serve the server shall stand with both feet at rest behind (*i.e.,* further from the net than) the base line, and within imaginary continuations of the center-mark and side line. The server shall then project the ball by hand into the air in any direction and *before it hits the ground* strike it with his racket, and the delivery shall be deemed to have been completed at the moment of the impact of the racket and the ball. A player with the use of only one arm may utilize his racket for the projection.

Case VI. Is it allowable in singles for the Server to stand behind the base line back of the alley?

Decision. No.

Case VII. May a player serve underhand?

Decision. Yes. There is no restriction regarding the kind of service which may be used; that is, the player may use an underhand or an overhand service at his discretion.

RULE 7 (FOOTFAULT RULE).—The Server shall throughout the delivery of the service—

(*a*) Not change his position by walking or running.

(*b*) Maintain contact with the ground.

(*c*) Keep both feet behind (*i.e.*, further from the net than) the base line.

Explanation of Rule 7

The following interpretation of Rule 7 was approved by the International Federation on March 15th, 1929:

(*a*) The Server shall not by the following movements of his feet be deemed "to change his position by walking or running," viz.:

(1) Slight movements of the feet which do not materially affect the location originally taken up by him.

(2) An unrestricted movement of one foot so long as the other foot maintains continuously its original contact with the ground.

(*b*) At no time during the delivery of the service (*i.e.*, from the taking up of the stance to the moment of impact of the racket and the ball—see Rule 6) may both feet be off the ground simultaneously.

(*c*) The word "feet" means the extremities of the legs below the ankles and at all times during the delivery of the service (as before described) every part of such extremities must be behind (*i.e.*, further from the net than) the base line.

RULE 8.—In delivering the service, the Server shall stand alternately behind the right and left courts, beginning from the right in every game. The ball served shall pass over the net and hit the ground within the service court which is diagonally opposite, or upon any line bounding such court, before the Receiver returns it.

Explanation of Rule 8

In the absence of a Linesman and Umpire, it is customary for the Receiver to determine whether the service is good or not.

It should be remembered, in handicap matches, that the Server starts to serve from the right-hand court no matter whether odds be given or owed.

RULE 9.—The service is a *Fault* (*a*) if the Server commit any breach of Rules 6, 7 or 8, (*b*) if he miss the ball in attempting to strike it, (*c*) if the ball served touch a permanent fixture (other than the net, strap or band) before it hits the ground.

Case VIII. After throwing the ball up preparatory to serving, the Server decides not to strike at it and catches it instead. Is it a fault?

Decision. No. He has not touched the ball "in attempting to strike it." The fact that he catches the ball shows that he has no longer any intention of delivering a service.

RULE 10.—After a fault (if it be the first fault) the Server shall serve again from behind the same half of the court from which he served that fault, unless it was a fault because he served from behind the wrong half, when he shall be entitled to deliver one service from behind the other half.

A fault may not be claimed after the next service has been delivered.

Case IX. A player serves from the wrong court; he loses the point, and then claims it was a fault.

Decision. The point stands as played.

Case X. The point score being 15-all, the Server by mistake serves from the left court; he wins the point and serves again, delivering a fault; the mistake is then discovered. Is he entitled to the previous point? From which court should he serve next?

Decision. The previous point stands. The next service should be from the left court, the score being 30-15 and the Server has served one fault.

Explanation of Rule 10

A service from the wrong court is a fault if discovered before the point is completed. If play on that point has been completed, the stroke stands as played whether the Server has won or lost. In either case, as soon as the mistake is discovered the Server must deliver his next serve from the proper court. All previous points before such discovery shall be scored as played. However, if the mistake of the Server was due to the incorrect calling of the score by the Umpire, the stroke should be declared a let and played over unless the point has been completed. The player should not suffer from the Umpire's error. (Case XXIV.)

RULE 11.—The Server shall not serve until the Receiver is ready. If the latter attempt to return the service, he shall be deemed ready. If, however, the Receiver signify that he is not ready, he may not claim a fault because the ball does not hit the ground within the limits fixed for the service.

CASE XI. The service is delivered before the Receiver is ready. He tries to return it and fails. Is he entitled to have it played over again?

Decision. No. If he attempts to return the service, he is deemed ready.

CASE XII. In receiving the service, a second ball was served while the first one (a let) was still in the air, and the two came in contact. No attempt was made to return the second service. The point was scored for the Server. Was this correct?

Decision. No. A let should be called.

CASE XIII. The Receiver calls "Not ready" for a second service. The ball strikes beyond the service line, and the Receiver claims that the fact that he was not ready makes no difference, since a fault cannot be returned, and, therefore, that two faults have been served.

Decision. The second service is a let. A player may not call "Not ready" and then have the service count, or not, as suits his interest.

Explanation of Rule 11

The Server must wait until the Receiver is ready for the second service as well as the first, and if the Receiver claims to be not ready and does not make any effort to return a service, the Server may not claim the point, even though the service was good.

RULE 12.—The service is a *Let* (a) if the ball served touch the net, strap or band, provided the same be otherwise good, (b) if a service or fault be delivered when the Receiver is not ready (see Rule 11). In case of a let, the service counts for nothing, and the Server shall serve again, but a let does not annul a previous fault.

Explanation of Rule 12

During the service, a ball that touches the net in going into the proper court is termed a let and counts for nothing, another service being delivered. If the ball touches the net when going into the proper court during a rally, it is good.

There is no limit to the number of let balls that may be made on the service, and the Server continues serving in the same court until a good service is delivered or two faults are made.

RULE 13.—At the end of the first game the Receiver shall become Server, and the Server, Receiver; and so on alternately in all the subsequent games of a match. If a player serve out of turn, the player who ought to have served shall serve as soon as the mistake is discovered. All points scored before such discovery shall be reckoned, but a single fault served before such discovery shall not be reckoned. If a game shall have been completed before such discovery, the order of service shall remain as altered.

RULE 14.—A ball is in play from the moment at which it is delivered in service (unless a fault or a let), and remains in play till the point is decided.

CASE XIV. A ball is played into the net; the player on the other side, thinking that the ball is coming over, strikes at it and hits the net. Who loses the point?

Decision. If the player touched the net while the ball was still in play, he loses the point. A ball touching the net ceases to be in play as soon as it is clear that the ball unimpeded will not cross the net.

RULE 15.—The Server wins the point (*a*) if the ball served touch the Receiver or anything which he wears or carries before it hits the ground, (*b*) if the Receiver otherwise lose the point as provided by Rule 17.

RULE 16.—The Receiver wins the point (*a*) if the Server serve two consecutive faults, (*b*) if the Server otherwise lose the point as provided by Rule 17.

RULE 17.—A player loses the point if—

(*a*) He fail, before the ball in play has hit the ground twice consecutively, to return it directly over the net [except as provided in Rule 20 (a) or (c)].

(*b*) He return the ball in play so that it hits the ground, a permanent fixture, or other object, outside any of the lines which bound his opponent's court [except as provided in Rule 20 (a) and 20 (c)]; or

(*c*) He volley the ball and fail to make a good return even when standing outside the court; or

(*d*) He touch or strike the ball in play with his racket more than once in making a stroke; or

(*e*) He or his racket (in his hand or otherwise) or anything which he wears or carries, touch the net, posts, cord or metal cable, strap or band, or the ground within his opponent's court at any time while the ball is in play; or

(*f*) He volley the ball before it has passed the net; or

(*g*) The ball in play touch him or anything that he wears or carries, except his racket in his hand or hands; or (*h*) He throw his racket at and hit the ball.

CASE XV. A player standing outside the court volleys the ball or catches it in his hand, and claims the stroke because the ball was certainly going out of court.

Decision. He loses the point. It makes no difference where he was standing. The return is presumed good until it strikes the ground outside of the court or a permanent fixture other than the net or posts.

CASE XVI. A player is struck by the ball served before it has touched the ground, he being outside of service court. How does it count?

Decision. The player struck loses the point. The service is presumably good until it strikes in the wrong court or out of court. A player may not take the decision upon himself by stopping the ball.

CASE XVII. In delivering a first service which falls outside the proper court, a player's racket slips out of his hand and flies into the net. Does he lose the point for hitting the net?

Decision. No; it counts merely as one fault whether the racket strikes the net before or after the ball falls outside.

RULE 18.—A ball falling on a line is regarded as falling in the court bounded by that line.

RULE 19.—If the ball in play touch a permanent fixture (other than the net, posts, cord or metal cable, strap or band) after it has hit the ground, the player who struck it wins the point; if before it hits the ground, his opponent wins the point.

CASE XVIII. A return hits the Umpire, or his chair or stand. The player claims that the ball was going into the court.

Decision. He loses the point.

Explanation of Rule 19

If a ball before touching the ground strikes the backstop, any of the officials or their chairs, the point is lost by the player who hit the ball. If, however, the ball strikes in the proper court and on the first bound hits any fixture (see Rule 2), the point is lost by the player receiving the ball.

RULE 20.—It is a good return—

(*a*) If the ball touch the net, posts, cord or metal cable, strap or band, provided that it passes over any of them and hits the ground within the court;

(*b*) If the ball, served or returned, hit the ground within the proper court and rebound or be blown back over the net, and the player whose turn it is to strike reach over the net and play the ball, provided that neither he nor any part of his clothes or racket touch the net, posts, cord or metal cable, strap or band or the ground within his opponent's court, and that the stroke be otherwise good;

(c) If the ball be returned outside the post, either above or below the level of the top of the net, even though it touch the post, provided that it hits the ground within the proper court;

(d) If a player's racket pass over the net after he has returned the ball, provided the ball pass the net before being played and be properly returned;

(e) If a player succeed in returning the ball, served or in play, which strikes a ball lying in the court.

NOTE—If for the sake of convenience a doubles court be equipped with singles posts for the purposes of a singles game, then the doubles posts and those portions of the net, cord or metal cable and band outside such singles posts shall *at all times* be permanent fixtures.

CASE XIX. Is it a good return if a player return the ball holding the racket in both hands?

Decision. Yes.

CASE XX. The service or the ball in play strikes a ball lying in the court. May it be returned?

Decision. Yes, if it is clear to the Umpire that the right ball is returned.

CASE XXI. A ball going out of court hits a net post and bounds into the opposite court. Is it a good return?

Decision. Yes.

Explanation of Rule 20

Should the ball touch a player while it is in play, no matter if the player is standing in or out of the court, he loses the point, and it should be remembered that a ball is good until it strikes the ground outside of the court. Should the player's racket touch the net, the posts or any part of them or if he steps into his opponent's court, or drops his racket into his opponent's court while the ball is still in play, he loses the point. If his racket strikes the ball before it comes over the net into his court, he loses the point. He may, however, strike the ball while it is in his court and permit his racket to follow the ball across the net without losing the point.

A ball hit with a sharp cut that bounds back over the net after having struck in the proper court is good. The player may reach over the net to return such a ball, but loses the point if he touches the net in doing so.

A return that passes between the net post and the net but below the top cord of the net is not a good return, because the net should fit flush to the net posts. The purpose of the net is to serve as a barrier, from post to post, between the players.

RULE 21.—In case a player is hindered in making a stroke by anything not within his control, except a permanent fixture of the court, the point shall be replayed.

CASE XXII. A spectator gets into the way of a player who fails to return the ball. May the player then claim a let?

Decision. Yes; if in the Umpire's opinion he was obstructed by a circumstance beyond his control. For instance, if the ropes or the seats are allowed to be so near to the court that a player is interfered with by them, the point should not be played again, because the ropes and seats form part of the arrangements of the ground. If, however, a spectator passes in front of those seats, or places a chair nearer than the original line, and so interferes with a player, the point should be played again.

CASE XXIII. A player is interfered with as above, and the Umpire directs the stroke to be played again. The Server had previously served a fault. Has he the right to two services?

Decision. No. The fault stands. A let does not annul a previous fault.

CASE XXIV. The Umpire or Linesman calls "Out," and then instantly changes and says "Play." The player fails to return the ball, and claims he was prevented by the Umpire.

Decision. The Umpire shall call a let, unless it is clear to him that the mistaken call was not in any way the cause of the player's failure to return the ball, in which case the point stands. In the case of a clear service ace, pass or placement, the point should not be replayed. Of course, where the final decision of the Linesman is "Out," a let should not be called in any case, but the player who struck the ball loses the point.

CASE XXV. During play a ball is thrown or comes into court and interferes with the play. What shall be done?

Decision. A let shall be called. But this shall apply only when the ball comes into court during play. It is the duty of the Receiver to remove loose balls from his court or to have them removed. If he fails to do so he must take the consequences.

CASE XXVI. The first ball served—a fault—strikes the backstop and returns, interfering with the Receiver at the time of the second service. May he claim a let?

Decision. Yes; but if he had an opportunity to remove the ball from the court, and negligently failed to do so, he may not claim a let.

CASE XXVII. During the play the Umpire calls "Let"; one of the players continues the point, wins it, and appeals to the Referee, who decided that the Umpire was in error as a matter of law in declaring a let. The player claims the point.

Decision. It is a let, unless the Umpire's erroneous call had no effect on the play.

Explanation of Rule 21

If a player, while the ball is in play, is interfered with by the gallery, by a ball coming into the court or by any disturbance not within his control, a let shall be called.

The Umpire is the judge of outside interference with the play, but in the case of a match played without officials, it is both courteous and customary to allow the player who is interfered with to decide.

RULE 22.—If a player wins his first point, the score is called 15 for that player; on winning his second point, the score is called 30 for that player; on winning his third point, the score is called 40 for that player; and the fourth point won by a player is scored *Game* for that player, except as follows:

If both players have won three points, the score is called *Deuce;* and the next point won by a player is scored *Advantage* for that player. If the same player wins the next point, he wins the game; if the other player wins the next point, the score is again called *Deuce;* and so on, until a player wins the two points immediately following the score at deuce, when the game is scored for that player.

Explanation of Rule 22

This method of scoring is the one used in all matches except when a handicap match is played under Tournament Regulation 23.

RULE 23.—The player who first wins six games wins a set, except as follows:

If both players have won five games, the score is called *Games-All,* and the next game won by a player is scored *Advantage Game* for that player. If the same player wins the next game, he wins the *Set;* if the other player wins the next game, the score is again called *Games-All;* and so on until a player wins two games more than his opponent, when the set is scored for that player.

RULE 24.—The players shall change sides at the end of the first, third and every subsequent alternate game of each set, and at the end of each set, unless the total number of games in such set be even, in which case the change is not made until the end of the first game of the next set.

Explanation of Rule 24

The change of courts is made after every *odd* game of each *set*. If the total number of games played in a set is even, play the first game of the next set in the same court in which the preceding set was finished; then change, play two games and change again, and so on.

If the number of games in a set is odd, change sides at the end of the set, play one game and change again.

Each set is considered as a separate unit.

It is the Umpire's duty to direct the competitors to change sides, in accordance with this law [Regulation 14 (e) of Tournament Regulations].

RULE 25.—The maximum number of sets in a match shall be five, or, where women take part, three.

RULE 26.—Except where otherwise stated, every reference in these Rules to the masculine includes the feminine gender.

RULE 27.—In matches where an Umpire is appointed, his decision shall be final; but where a Referee is appointed, an appeal shall lie to him from the decision of an Umpire on a question of law, and in all such cases the decision of the Referee shall be final.

The Referee, in his discretion, may at any time postpone a match on account of darkness or the condition of the ground or the weather. In any case of postponement the previous score and the previous occupancy of courts shall hold good, unless the Referee and the players unanimously agree otherwise.

Explanation of Rule 27

The Referee postpones the match or approves of such action on the part of the Umpire. [Tournament Regulations 10 and 14 (g).]

In case of a postponement the match is resumed from the point, game and set score existing when the match was stopped, *unless* the Referee and both players unanimously agree to play the entire match, or any part of it, over.

RULE 28.—Play shall be continuous from the first service till the match be concluded; provided that after the third set, or when women take part, the second set, either player is entitled to a rest, which shall not exceed ten minutes, except that in the countries situated between Latitude 15° North and Latitude 15° South such rest shall not exceed forty-five minutes,* and provided further that when necessitated by circumstances not within the control of the players, the Umpire may suspend play for such a period as he may consider necessary. If play be suspended and be not resumed until a later day the rest may be taken only after the third set (or when women take part, the second set) of play on such later day, completion of an unfinished set being counted one set. These provisions shall be strictly construed, and play shall never be suspended, delayed or interfered with for the purpose of enabling a player to recover his strength or his wind or to receive instruction or advice. The Umpire shall be the sole judge of such suspension, delay or interference, and after giving due warning he may disqualify the offender.

Explanation of Rule 28

In men's events there is no rest in a two out of three set match, but in a three out of five set match, a ten-minute rest may be taken only after the third set. It may not be taken before the third set or at any time after the fourth set has been started. It must be taken after the third set or not at all.

In women's matches a rest of ten minutes may be taken after the second set or not at all.

All matches for Juniors shall be the best two out of three sets with no rest. In the case of Tennis Center Championships or Interscholastic, State and Sectional Tournaments, equivalent to Tennis Centers, and in National Junior Championships the final round shall be the best three out of five sets. If such final requires more than three sets to decide, there must be a rest of ten minutes after the third set.

Matches for boys and girls shall be the best two out of three sets and there must be a ten-minute rest after the second set.

The players must be back on the court ten minutes after play has ceased.

Should a player, on account of physical unfitness or an unavoidable accident, not within his control, be unable to continue play, he must be defaulted.

"Stalling" is one of the hardest things to deal with. The rules say that "play shall be continuous." An Umpire should determine whether the "stalling" is deliberate and for the purpose of gaining time. If he decides that it is, he should warn the player to stop his unfair practice; if this does not end it, he should then default him.

The Umpire has the power to suspend a match for such period as he may think necessary, if, in his judgment, the play is interfered with by circumstances beyond the players' control. Such circumstances might be the passing of an airplane, moving of spectators in the stands, etc.

---

* NOTE—Any Nation is at liberty to modify the first provision in Rule 28, or omit it from its regulations governing tournaments, matches or competitions held in its own country, other than the International Lawn Tennis Championship (Davis Cup).

THE DOUBLES GAME

RULE 29.—The foregoing rules shall apply to the *Doubles Game* except as follows:

RULE 30.—For the doubles game, the court shall be 36 feet in width, *i.e.*, 4½ feet wider on each side than the court for the singles game, and those portions of the singles side lines which lie between the two service lines shall be called the *Service Side Lines*. In other respects the court shall be similar to that described in Rule 1, but the portions of the singles side lines between the base line and the service line on each side of the net may be omitted if desired.

CASE XXVIII. In doubles the Server claims the right to stand at the corner of the court as marked by the doubles side line. Is the foregoing correct or is it necessary that the Server stand within the limits of the center mark and the singles side line?

Decision. The Server has the right to stand anywhere between the center mark and the doubles side lines.

RULE 31.—The pair who have to serve in the first game of each set shall decide which partner shall do so, and the opposing pair shall decide similarly for the second game. The partner of the player who served in the first game shall serve in the third; the partner of the player who served in the second game shall serve in the fourth, and so on in the same order in all the subsequent games of a set. The order of service having been decided shall not be altered during the set, but it may be changed at the beginning of a new set.

CASE XXIX. In doubles, one player does not appear in time to play, and his partner claims to be allowed to play single-handed against the opposing pair. May he do so?

Decision. No.

Explanation of Rule 31

At the start of any new set a pair may change the order of service from that followed in the preceding set. This order may not be changed during a set.

It is optional with them which shall serve first, but they must serve alternately throughout each set.

RULE 32.—The pair who have to receive the service in the first game of each set shall decide which partner shall receive the first service and the opposing pair shall decide similarly in the second game of each set. Partners shall receive the service alternately throughout each game and the order of receiving the service having been decided shall not be altered during the set, but it may be changed at the beginning of a new set.

Case XXX. Is it allowable, in doubles, for a partner of the Server to stand in the center of the service court, and thereby obstruct the view of the Receiver?

Decision. Yes. The partner may take any position in the court that he wishes.

Explanation of Rule 32

The receiving formation of a doubles team may not be changed during a set; only at the start of a new set. Partners must receive throughout each set on the same sides of the court which they originally select when the set begins. The first Server is not required to receive in the right court; he may select either side, but must hold this to the end of the set.

RULE 33.—If a partner serve out of his turn, the partner who ought to have served shall serve as soon as the mistake is discovered, but all points scored, and any fault served before such discovery, shall be reckoned. If a game shall have been completed before such discovery, the order of service remains as altered.

Explanation of Rule 33

A point or game that has been played out and finished stands, even though the wrong partner has served. The match goes on as though no error had been committed, the partner who did not serve out of turn serving next.

RULE 34.—If during a game the order of receiving the service is changed by the receivers it shall remain as altered until the end of the game in which the mistake is discovered, but the partners shall resume their original order of receiving in the next game of that set in which they are receivers of the service.

RULE 35.—The service is a fault as provided for by Rule 9, or if the ball served touch the Server's partner or anything which he wears or carries; but if the ball served touch the partner of the Receiver or anything which he wears or carries, before it hits the ground, the Server wins the point.

RULE 36.—The ball shall be struck alternately by one or other player of the opposing pairs, and if a player touch the ball in play with his racket in contravention of this Rule, his opponents win the point.

CASE XXXI. In doubles a ball is struck at by a player at the net, and also by his partner, both players missing the ball, which drops outside the court. Neither player called "Out." Who wins the point?

Decision. The point goes to the players who struck at the ball and missed it. An unsuccessful attempt to hit the ball, or calling "Out," has no bearing on the case.

CPSIA information can be obtained
at www.ICGtesting.com
Printed in the USA
BVHW050719210122
626661BV00003B/43